The
Intimate
Connection

Does any of this feel or sound familiar?

- You can't remember the last time you had a conversation—just the two of you.
- You've forgotten what the tinglies of first love felt like.
- The line you hate hearing most is, "You just don't understand. You'll never understand."
- Your former passionate kiss before work has turned into a flung "See you" as you run out the door.
- Your spouse is nothing like the intriguing man or woman you thought you married. He or she is more like . . . your sibling.
- The most meaningful words you've said to your spouse lately were, "Did you get OJ?"
- You wish you knew what your spouse's hot buttons were . . . before you pressed them.
- You dread the heavy sigh and the comment, "But that's not the way my dad did it."
- Holding hands is a distant memory.
- The one you want to be closest to is your spouse, but you don't know how to accomplish that.
- Sometimes the two of you are like oil and water—you simply don't mix.
- Your "dating behavior" has gone out the window.
- One or both of you need a healthy dose of anger management.
- An attempt to talk results only in a grunt during TV commercials.
- Your bedroom resembles the arctic tundra during winter.
- You wish your spouse truly understood the pressure you were always under to be perfect.

- You need a linguistics class to understand what your spouse is really saying.
- You wish that for once she'd pay as much attention to you as she does to the neighbors.
- A romantic evening is watching someone else kiss in a movie.
- You never say what you feel, because you don't want to rock the boat.
- His silence speaks volumes, but you're not sure how to get him to talk.
- You lie awake at night thinking, *Isn't there more to a life together than this?*

If you've thought any of the above, rest assured, you're not the only one. Millions of husbands and wives across the planet have at some point in their marriage.

But you don't have to settle for less-than, blah, or a battlefield in your relationship. You can have the intimate connection you long for.

This book will help you:

- understand each other's needs and backgrounds
- communicate in ways your spouse will really listen to
- develop deep, meaningful, satisfying, and long-lasting intimacy as a couple

I guarantee it.

The

Intimate Connection

SECRETS *to a*
LIFELONG ROMANCE

DR. KEVIN LEMAN

Revell

a division of Baker Publishing Group
Grand Rapids, Michigan

248.844
Leman

Library of Congress Cataloging-in-Publication Data
Names: Leman, Kevin, author.
Title: The intimate connection : secrets to a lifelong romance / Dr. Kevin Leman.
Description: Grand Rapids : Revell, a division of Baker Publishing Group, 2019. |
    Includes bibliographical references.
Identifiers: LCCN 2018052086 | ISBN 9780800734947 (pbk.)
Subjects: LCSH: Marriage—Religious aspects—Christianity.
Classification: LCC BV835 .L46 2019 | DDC 248.8/44—dc23
LC record available at https://lccn.loc.gov/2018052086

To my wife, Bucky—
Still my best gift ever.

Contents

Acknowledgments

Grateful thanks to:

My Revell team.
My longtime editor, Ramona Cramer Tucker.

Introduction

How to Get Now What You Had Back Then

Think back a little, or a lot—depending on how long you and your spouse have been together—to those first days when you were falling in love. Remember those euphoric tinglies? That intense desire to learn all you could about each other? The fairy-tale time when you couldn't wait to talk to each other, to hug each other, to spend every moment possible together, and it was the two of you united against the world?

Contrast that with the present day. Does the following scenario sound all too familiar?

It's a typical Friday night, and every member of the family is running out the door to separate destinations. You're an unusual family if you were able to fit in dinner together before the great split happened.

You've managed to pick up your two younger kids from school after your part-time job. After a quick dinner, compliments of Colonel Sanders, you're dropping 15-year-old Jessica off at the movie theater and 11-year-old Alex at a friend's house to hang out. Your 17-year-old is driving himself to his football game. You'll get there by the end of the first quarter if you hurry.

Your husband is working late on a project so he will hightail it straight to the game. The only time you've "talked" to him today was during a brief exchange of who will be where, and when. After the game, you'll pick up the two younger kids at their locations while he heads home for tepid leftovers.

You know exactly what to expect when you get home—a trashed living room from the week, a kitchen sink piled high with dishes, and laundry creeping out of your teens' bedrooms. You sigh as you drive home, estimating how long the nuclear fallout will take to clean up so that you can fall into bed. You know you won't be able to sleep before you clean up the mess, because you don't want to face it first thing tomorrow morning. And you need to be in the car by 9:00 for Alex's soccer practice.

Life today is fast-paced and complicated, isn't it?

If you're like most couples, the euphoric "I'm in love" feelings and deluge of sweet time together just being in each other's presence have turned into a dizzying swirl of grocery runs, long workdays, barely saying hello in the morning before you rush separate ways, and tucking the kids into bed before you fall asleep, exhausted.

Somewhere along the way, you may feel like you've lost each other. Your communication has become routine and mundane. You no longer have time for those long walks hand in hand to share your hearts, goals, and dreams. That partner who was once exciting to you now might look a little bland. You may even wonder as you lie awake at night, *Isn't there more to marriage and a life together than this?*

But imagine that after that crazy Friday, you walked in the door and this sight greeted you instead: Your kitchen is spotless—dishes done, counter wiped, garbage taken out. Your living room is picked up, and the pillows are even aligned on the couch. You peek in the laundry room, and the laundry has been sorted and there's a load already in the washer. There's even a red candle glowing in the kitchen with a note beside it:

I love you, hon. There's another surprise waiting for you in the bathroom.

You peek in the bathroom door. The usually trashed room has transformed into a beautiful spa. Your fuzziest towel—a red rose adorning it—and a bottle of chilled water are by the tub. You inhale the lovely lavender scent of the bubble bath your man has drawn for you. Then you spot another note:

Just relax. I'll take care of everything.

A strange notion hits you: *Is this really my house?*

Yes, it's your house. But an amazing transformation has taken place because of the secrets I'll share with you in this book. That same transformation is possible for you and your spouse, when you understand each other's needs and learn to communicate in ways each of you will understand and accept. That's what this book is all about—creating a long-lasting, intimate connection.

In the chapters ahead, we'll

- unravel the complex needs of men and women
- discover who your spouse really is
- look at the warning signs of relational breakdown that may be creeping into your marriage
- explore how the backgrounds and birth orders of you and your spouse impact how you react to each other and to situations differently
- reveal the best ways to communicate—ways your spouse will listen to
- learn how you can best show love to your unique spouse
- grapple with healthy ways to deal with anger and frustration
- determine how to short-circuit the destructive games couples unwittingly play and turn them into positive, relationship-building activities

- give you ideas and an "I Promise" Challenge for building, regaining, and keeping intimacy in your marriage long-term

If you're reading this book, you picked it up because you crave a more satisfying marriage. You don't want to be just roommates who only intersect over the basic necessities of life and television reruns.

Perhaps you long for sweet touches, for a stimulating flow of conversation, and to share your days and dreams with the kind of life partner you've always dreamed of. Or, frankly, you know your marriage is on rocky ground and you want to do what you can to save it. Or perhaps you just got married, feel like the honeymoon ended too soon, and want to do what you can to make your marriage what you dreamed it would be.

No matter what your relationship with your spouse is right now, you can have the lifelong intimacy you longed for when you were dating or said "I do." *The Intimate Connection* reveals how.

Ready to get the marriage you deserve? Let's plunge in.

SECRET #1

Acts of Love Create an Unbreakable Bond

If you want to change your spouse, try changing yourself first.

Flash back to that busy Friday for a minute, where you've been running yourself ragged all day, and you know there's a mess for you to tackle at home. Then you walk in the door and *voila!* A mess-free living room and sparkly clean kitchen await you. Don't forget that romantic surprise in the bathroom too.

Ladies, how would you feel at that moment? I bet most of you can relate to the first "messy" part of the story. You've been there, done that, and sighed every night you've seen it. But when I got to the part about the dishes washed, the living room picked up, and the first load of laundry in the washer, you likely rolled your eyes and said, "Oh, I thought this was a *true* story."

Gentlemen, if you're the one reading this book, you might have felt a bit uncomfortable. Many of you can relate to the working-hard-all-day concept and then running somewhere to a kid's activity.

By the time you finally get home, you're starving and exhausted. The last thing you can think of is more work, like cleaning up the house. That's especially true if there was a strong division of male and female roles in the house you grew up in.

You might have been romantic once—to turn your bride's attention and affection to you instead of any other males who were interested in her. But once you said "I do," you figured you got the job done . . . and done well. After all, you captured the prize—the special lady you wanted to spend a lifetime with. Romance is no longer the first thing on your mind because you've already accomplished that mission. Now you have to focus on other competitive things, like jostling for positions with others in your field so you can grow your career and put food on your family's table.

An intimate connection doesn't just happen without effort on both your parts. It includes expressions of love— sacrificial acts of giving—that reveal an understanding of each other's unique needs and desires.

But an intimate connection doesn't just happen without effort on both your parts. It includes expressions of love—sacrificial acts of giving—that reveal an understanding of each other's unique needs and desires. The most intimate of all acts—sex—is the culmination of the couple's continual, shared closeness. It's most definitely not gained through the game of "I'm Tarzan, you Jane— gimme," or vice versa. That sort of relationship is one-sided, is unfulfilling to both parties, and likely won't last.

But a husband and wife who can communicate well and share such deep intimacy that they want to do acts of love for each other? Now that's an unbreakable bond.

Want to Change Your Spouse?

Most people want to change their spouse but aren't willing to do the work to change themselves. As a wise coach I know once told me, "They don't care what you know until they know you care." Here's what I mean.

Ladies, if you were the one who walked into that clean space on a Friday night, you'd also likely walk back out of the house and check the number on the door to make sure it was your place and that you hadn't unwittingly entered someone else's in your tiredness. When you walk back inside and see your husband switching the load of wash for you, something magical will happen. You'll get stars in your eyes. Romantic music will begin to play in your head. Your house will suddenly feel like a castle. You'll feel like a princess.

That man of yours will never look more like a knight in shining armor than at that moment. You know he understands your needs and is going out of his way to meet them because he loves and treasures you. He may have a balding spot on the back of his head, and his abs may not be what they were 10 years ago, but suddenly he's the romantic figure of your dreams . . . and incredibly sexy.

Intimacy truly is an all-day affair. And it starts with communication and understanding each other's needs and desires.

That's why I've always said that marital intimacy doesn't begin in the bedroom. It starts in the laundry room, the kitchen, and anywhere else you two intersect. Intimacy truly is an all-day affair. And it starts with communication and understanding each other's needs and desires.

Meet Rob and Maria

Rob worked long hours at a newly launched office downtown, then headed home to his wife, Maria, and their toddler. Formerly a full-time nurse at a local hospital, Maria now worked four nights a week so she could be at home with their daughter, Emily, during the day. She also paid their bills and handled the calls for any home repairs.

In spite of her sleep deprivation and the exhaustion of dealing with their active youngster, Maria managed to pull off a home-cooked dinner some of those nights. And each night she'd welcome Rob home with a kiss and ask him about his day.

He never asked about hers. He'd simply grunt a perfunctory "Fine," then head to the shower. She'd simultaneously finish cooking dinner and keep their daughter occupied so he had time to de-stress.

Over dinner, when she asked if he liked the new Crock-Pot dish she'd tried that day, he'd grunt, "Yeah."

She'd tell him a funny thing their daughter did that day.

His response? Grunt #3.

She'd mention a milestone at work.

Grunt #4.

After that, talk would shut down. Maria knew it was purposeless.

With dinner finished, Rob's routine was to plop on the couch and watch TV while Maria did the dishes, gave Emily a bath, and got her ready for bed.

From Rob's perspective, he'd already done his day's work. Since his wife only worked part-time, it was only right that she take care of the kid and the housework. That way they were even, he figured, and he didn't think anything else about it. After all, his mom had always been home and took care of him and his brother as they were growing up.

But inside Maria a cauldron of resentment was growing. What had happened to the romantic guy who gave her flowers and opened the car door when they were dating? Now she felt like Velcro Woman—with every family task and responsibility sticking to her.

Her husband had turned from being the helpful partner she thought she'd have into a couch-potato teenager wannabe. He avoided all responsibility by passing the buck for anything that happened at home to his exhausted wife.

Guys, I'll shoot it to you straight. If Rob's actions sound anything like yours, it's time for you to man up. There are two in this marriage, and you both need to pull your weight in the household chores. If you have kids, it took two of you to create them, so two of you should be responsible for them.

Scenarios involving lack of communication and lack of caring about each other's feelings play out all across America every day.

Just being a mom is a 24-7 job, even without a part-time job to boot. And women who work *outside* the home return from their jobs to work *inside* the home. They've essentially got a double job. Yet, because many men don't understand that relationship basic, scenarios involving lack of communication and lack of caring about each other's feelings play out all across America every day.

Rob and Maria, Three Years Later

Maria's frustrations came to a head after their daughter's kindergarten open house. The next week, she came to see me.

"He's so insensitive and thoughtless. He never takes how I feel into consideration," she told me.

She'd asked Rob numerous times to go with her, since it was after his work hours. But he'd told her, "It's just kindergarten. All they do is play anyway. It's not like it's serious work. You go. You're taking the kid, right? I could use some quiet." Then he'd gone back to his channel surfing.

That night she'd fixed a quick supper of hamburgers after juggling kindergarten paperwork and a medical checkup for their daughter in the afternoon. She didn't have time to clean up the kitchen before she and Emily left for the school's open house.

When they arrived home at 8:30 p.m., Rob was still slouched in his favorite chair, watching a Monday night football game. He didn't say, "Hi, hon, I'm glad you're home," or ask how the evening had gone. He didn't even acknowledge their return.

Then Maria walked into the kitchen. Not only had Rob not done the dishes but he hadn't made a single move toward straightening anything up. The lids weren't back on the mustard or mayo jars. A sticky knife and wadded-up napkins rested on the counter. Nothing had been put back in the refrigerator, including a half gallon of milk, which was now room temperature. The slices of cheese, lettuce, tomato, and onion—not a good odor after two hours—limply rested on the same plate she'd put them out on.

"I was angry," she told me. "Enough that I made a little noise putting things away in the kitchen."

"Just a *little* noise?" I asked her. I was surprised she hadn't marched back into that living room and launched her couch potato off that couch. It would certainly have been tempting.

But Maria was the epitome of self-control and used to being the sacrificial lamb of their family. So she banged the fridge door a few times. She clanged the silverware. She even stomped between her husband and his TV screen to take the garbage bag out the front door, instead of going out the kitchen door as usual. Then she tucked their new kindergartener in bed and read her a story.

By the time Maria had finished, she was furious and exhausted. All she wanted was to crash into bed and not wake up until morning. Pulling the covers up to her chin, she rolled to the very edge of her side of the bed . . . as far away as she could get from him.

Fifteen minutes later, both Monday night football and the news were over. Her husband shot her that Bullwinkle the Moose gaze, climbed into bed, and snuggled next to her.

When she stiffened and tried to move even farther away, he tried to sweet-talk her with the six words no woman wants to hear: "Geez, what's the matter with you?"

In seconds, the atmosphere surrounding both husband and wife in that bedroom resembled the arctic before any glacial melting.

But here's what's fascinating. Though Rob had acted insensitively for years, Maria came to see me because she wasn't ready to give up on him yet. She said she still loved him, even though most of the time she wasn't exactly sure why. She wanted to know if there were ways she could change him . . . and their relationship. She longed for the kind of intimate connection she had dreamed they'd have when they got married.

"You can't change another person," I told her. "That's up to them. But you can make some changes in your own responses, which might prompt him to make changes in the way he responds to you."

Is that easy? No, especially if the other person is someone like Rob, Mr. Couch Potato, and you seem like the one doing all the work. But if you could get the mutually satisfying marriage you dream of, isn't that worth your best shot and a little bit of work on the front end?

Change Starts with You

If you want to change someone else's behavior, you have to start by changing your own behavior first. Handing your spouse this book and saying, "Here, I think you should read this because you need it" won't do either of you any good. It will just anger your spouse and shut them down.

But if you read this book and demonstrate by your own actions—little things that show your spouse how much you care—that you want to make things better between the two of you, I guarantee you'll see a steady improvement in your marriage.

If you want to change someone else's behavior, you have to start by changing your own behavior first.

Relationships are not like microwaves, though. They can't instantly produce a product. If there is a long history of not communicating, ignoring each other's needs, and having some distance wedged between you, one act of love and some sweet words won't be enough to convince your spouse you mean business and are determined for things to change. But slowly, steadily, as you focus on the principles in this book, the everyday changes you're making will transform your heart and actions and make their way into your spouse's heart and actions.

Right now you might feel a little like Maria and need some pointers to get your relationship turned around and headed in the right direction. Or perhaps the disconnect between you and your spouse is enough that you're ready to toss your marital towel out of the ring and call the match over. Maybe your communication isn't as good as you think it could be, or you have a few difficulties you'd like to work out. Or your relationship simply feels bland and boring, and you'd like to make it more mutually satisfying.

Wherever you and your spouse are in the above descriptions, or if you're somewhere in between, let me encourage you. It *is* possible to create a marriage where the two of you mutually respect each other, desire to please each other, are sensitive and tuned-in to each other's needs, and consider the other your number-one priority in life. It all starts with communication skills, adds acts

MAN to MAN

Helping your wife with the myriad things she does (many of them for you) isn't being a wuss. It's being the manly rock she needs and deserves to count on. Nothing's more attractive than a man who has dishpan hands and does little somethings that make his wife and her girlfriends say, "Aw, how sweet."

You may have been married for 20 years, but your wife still has a girly side. When you show her sensitivity and thoughtfulness—taking into account her feelings and the fact she's Velcro Woman, with multiple people and responsibilities sticking to her—you are truly a MAN.

So be that knight in shining armor, her very personal fairy tale come true. Light a candle, roll up those sleeves, and handwrite a love note. You'll be glad you did.

of love, and moves outward to grow intimacy in all areas of life, including emotional and sexual needs.

The Essential Ingredient—Motivation

How can you have the love-of-a-lifetime relationship you long for and deserve? Where you are free to share intimate thoughts and feelings without fear of judgment? Where you understand each other's backgrounds and the ways they affect how you express love? Where you think first of the other person and not what you'll get from them?

It starts with the critical ingredient of motivation. Your spouse is the one who knows you best, and any false motives will be spotted a mile or more away.

If a guy thinks, *Hey, if I clean up the apartment, maybe I'll get some action tonight*, his actions will backfire because he doesn't have the right motivation. But if he comes home to a messy apartment and thinks, *Wow, we've both worked hard this week. I bet she'd love to come home and have it clean. That would make her so happy*, then he's on the right track.

What will his happy wife think? *What an amazing man I married. I'm so glad I married him. He's just the best. And he's mine.* The next time she's on the phone with a girlfriend, she sings his praises, fully knowing her husband is listening.

That wonderful man might even be rewarded with a surprise bonus—his favorite home-cooked dinner the next week when his wife gets home early from work, or a nice roll in the sack with her on the soft rug in that cleaned-up living room.

See how it works?

We all long for connection. Yet today many husbands and wives live a married-singles lifestyle. They meet and connect on the basics just because they reside in the same location and share a refrigerator. But husband and wife live their own separate lives— including work, friends, and hobbies. In many of those homes,

FOR
WOMEN ONLY

Your girlfriend just got two free tickets to a movie premiere on the night you and your husband have set aside as a date night. What would you do?

Option A: Go with your girlfriend, because you know your husband will understand. After all, it's free, and it's a great opportunity to spend time with someone you enjoy.

Option B: Turn the offer down nicely since you have previous plans.

Option C: Tell your friend you're unavailable that night because you have previous plans, but ask her if there is any other available showtime.

What did you decide?

Your response is a litmus test for your relationship. Is your husband your first priority, or is that friend?

If you chose option A, you might have a fun evening. But you'll hurt your marriage in the long run. Your guy won't likely say it, but his feelings will be a little hurt. Even if he tells you, "That's okay. Go ahead. Sounds like a fun night," don't do it. It's a step on the road to disconnection. If you're not willing to say no to something you want to do in order to spend time with your husband, you're starting down a slippery slope. There's no magic dust here. To stay connected, you have to make time together a priority.

I'm not talking about just doing routine activities together—like bowling or watching movies. On activity-driven dates like that, you're more likely to talk about your hook or slice or the movie plot than each other. So why not try a simple picnic or stroll around the block as a replacement? Anything that leads you and that man you love to talk, connect your hearts, and get on the same page.

If you chose option B and told your guy, "Ellie had movie premiere tickets for tomorrow night, but I turned her down. I want to spend time with you, and it's our special night," he'll be smiling for a week, thinking about what a lucky guy he is to have married you.

If you chose option C, you'll have both a happy guy *and* a fun night out with a friend.

It wasn't that hard to do, was it?

(If you're a guy who's sneak-reading this, the same exact advice goes to you.)

nothing at all happens behind bedroom doors, or it occurs only as a "duty," like doing the laundry on Saturdays. Their romantic relationship is hardly the culmination of an entire day full of affection, consideration, love, and unity.

All marriages have bright spots and some negative moments or days. However, if you picked up this book because the number of distant or dissatisfied days is growing, then kudos to you. You're smart to catch your relationship in time before you start sliding downhill. Many spouses have root problems in their marriages—ones we'll discuss in this book—that they try to cover over by spending time with everyone except their spouse. To turn things around, you have to put the brakes on for a while, evaluate what's happening and what each of you really needs, and then begin to roll down the marital road positively from there.

Acts motivated by love will produce all kinds of long-lasting dividends in your relationship.

Acts motivated by love will produce all kinds of long-lasting dividends in your relationship. Those acts mean, "You're so important to me that I will do anything I can to make life more pleasurable for you." Such acts create a contented, loving, grateful atmosphere in your home that will drive the two of you back into each other's arms time and again and divorce-proof your marriage.

If your husband has your back and steps in to help when you're feeling stressed, you're not going to look twice at the handsome new assistant in your office.

If your wife greets you with a kiss in spite of your kids' shenanigans, genuinely shows interest in what matters most to you, and whispers in your ear, "I'm so lucky I married you," even with sticky strawberry jelly on her sleeve from making PB&Js, she'll be more attractive to you than any other hottie you might encounter.

Can your marriage become one like that? Yes, it can! This book will give you the road map to renewing your relationship so that your marriage can become the mutually satisfying, fulfilling love of a lifetime that you dream of. But first, you'll have to take a few risks:

- opening your heart and mind to surprising revelations about your preconceived notions . . . that you had no idea you have
- taking a good look at yourself and your background, as well as your spouse's
- realizing how the unique backgrounds of you and your spouse influence your way of thinking and subsequent behaviors, both individually and where you intersect as a couple

Most of us don't truly understand ourselves, so how can we understand our spouse? And without that understanding, it's nearly impossible to truly become one in marriage. So you must be able to recognize your own feelings and identify why you do what you do—you've been preconditioned, most of the time without your knowledge. However, with the powerful answers you'll receive from the revelations in this book, you'll be able to reprogram even gut reactions to proactive responses that will grow your relationship with your spouse.

But keep in mind that a book is just a book. It can give you time-tested advice and ideas, but you and your spouse are the ones who have to commit to trying out some of them, as well as inventing your own. Also, every relationship is unique because it's comprised of two individuals from two unique backgrounds. Depending on those backgrounds and where you are in your relationship, some of the ideas in this book will be perfectly suited to you. Others you might decide to take a pass on.

I encourage you to personalize this book. Highlight and pursue ideas you like. I know the suggestions here work, because they've transformed the relationships of hundreds of thousands of couples. The examples I've included are based on real stories of couples I've counseled. However, every piece of advice won't apply to every reader. So if you run across advice that doesn't apply to or fit you, cross it out or skip those pages. I won't mind. Relationships are handmade. What's important is that you make this book your own and that you follow through on the actions needed to bring about changes in your marriage.

Do it for yourself.

Do it for your spouse.

And do it for your kids, your "someday" kids, or those youngsters around you who are continually watching.

SECRET #2

Outside Forces Have Shaped Your Relationship (without Your Permission)

Three societal factors that greatly impact how you think, feel, and relate to your spouse.

When you hear the word *marriage*, what's the first thing you think of?

For many in today's world, the word *love* rarely comes to mind—or, if it does, it's a contradiction.

Take the 30-something lawyer who was having a rough day. After catching an earful for having typos in an email to her boss, she forgot to bring an important document to court. Then she dropped her cell phone in the standing water in the restroom sink.

"What's the matter with you?" her law partner teased. "Are you in love or something?"

"Of course I'm not in love," she snapped back. "I'm married."

How sad, but true of so many couples.

Then there's the 11-year-old boy who was asked by a neighbor, "Hey, is your older sister still dating that guy? They seemed so happy and in love."

"Not anymore," he shot back. "They hardly even talk to each other."

"Oh," the neighbor said. "Sorry to hear they broke up."

The boy shook his head. "They didn't break up. They got married."

Many people today think that if you want to take the romance out of a relationship, just slip a wedding ring on. Reality hits and the magic pixie dust disappears. It's not a surprise that many people are schooled to think that. After all, they've seen how their parents related to each other, and they've failed a round or two in marriage themselves.

A troubled woman once told me, "My mom and dad have always been like separate planets. They have their own orbits and never intersect. They never talk to each other. They never touch each other. They've never shown any love to each other." It's no wonder she was having trouble connecting with her husband.

Top off any relational disconnect with the way society disses males and females and talks cynically about marriage, and you're assaulted with a constant bombardment of negativity. Such negativity contributes to the disconnect you're feeling, whether you realize it or not. Understanding how three societal factors affect you, your partner, and multiple areas where you intersect is a positive first step in resolving misunderstandings and getting you on the same page with the one you love.

#1: Redefined Gender Roles

Male and female roles used to be tightly defined by society, and few spoke out against the status quo for fear of social ostracism. With the redefining and homogenizing of roles, more and more women have left home and entered the workplace, whether full-time or part-time.

Some men who had previously been secure in their roles of protector and provider became confused about their roles. Threatened by the female push for independence and drive for equality, they became defensive and insecure. Were they no longer needed by the women in their lives? Did they no longer have a social role? How could they fit the role of the "softer male"—one who was more gentle, more romantic, and more . . . well, everything they weren't sure how to be? What about their natural drive to compete and protect? Was that wrong or no longer needed? Such confusion left men flailing to find a new identity as women pushed forward in their newfound freedom.

Am I suggesting we go back to the dark ages in human history, where male and female roles were strictly defined and immovable? Absolutely not. For America to remain the land of the free, with every individual retaining "unalienable rights," a broader perspective and understanding of changing roles is necessary. But I'm pointing this out to highlight that societal change and the resulting upheaval in male and female roles still wreak havoc in relationships.

You see, instilled in every male psyche is this underlying thought: *I'm the knight who has to kill the dragon to rescue the fair damsel in distress.* It's not just in the storybooks. Yet doing this in today's world isn't always welcomed by females, who want to be taken seriously in their own right.

Instilled in every male psyche is this underlying thought: **I'm the knight who has to kill the dragon to rescue the fair damsel in distress.**

The other day I did something for a woman that my mama taught me to do—open the door for her. But I didn't get a thank-you. Instead, the young lady snapped, "I can do that myself, thank you very much."

Even though I've lived a long time in this world, such a verbal slap was deflating to someone who simply wanted to extend a kind, manly gesture. I was understandably confused. After all, when as a psychologist

35

I ask women what they really want in a guy, I hear these types of things:

"I want him to treat me like I'm a treasure."

"I want to feel like a girl when I'm next to him."

"I want him to hold my hand and open doors for me."

"I want to feel safe and protected."

I don't think I've ever heard:

"I want him to talk to me like an acquaintance."

"I want him to treat me like one of the guys."

"I don't want him to do stupid stuff like opening doors for me. I can do that myself, thank you very much."

"I want him to let me fight my own battles."

At the core of a woman is the innate desire to be loved and treated like a treasure. However, what a woman says or does and what she means are often two very different things. And behind every statement or action is a life mantra. The young lady who snapped at me likely had had difficult experiences with males—whether a father, stepfather, or boyfriend—and thus had lost her trust in men. So she'd adopted a tough core that screamed to the world, "I don't need you" and "I'll show you I don't need you. Just watch me."

Behind every statement or action is a life mantra.

After that experience with the young woman, I thought, *No wonder most guys don't open doors for women anymore. They're not secure enough to try. They're afraid they'll be slammed.*

The same is true for husbands in marriage. Sometimes they're not secure enough to try—especially if their wives look like they are juggling everything in their lives capably, at least on the surface.

Women can be terribly intimidating because they are so good at doing so many things simultaneously (unlike us men, who tend to focus on one thing at a time to conquer it). Not only does my wife, Sande, make incredible meals, but she's also a delightful hostess and keeps up with our five kids, three sons-in-law, and four grand-kids simultaneously. For many years, she even ran her own store.

Then there's me. Some days I can't remember where I put my car keys. But there's one thing I can always do better than Sande— pry the lid off the pickle jar.

Though men and women are absolute social equals, men tra-ditionally have been physically stronger than women. Yes, I've seen some female bodybuilders, and I wouldn't want to get into an arm-wrestling competition with any of them. I know hands down they'd win. However, I still feel manly when I can use my physical strength to help the wife I love.

I believe a man's protective nature is instinctive. In ancient times physical dangers surrounded a family on all sides—wild animals, enemy tribesmen, you name it—so the male was forced into the role of hunter, warrior, and protector. It was a survival-challenge reality show to the extreme. If you didn't compete, and compete well, you were toast.

That role of protector is still embedded within most males to some degree today—in spite of society's attempt to homogenize male and female roles. If you don't believe me, take a look at the animal world.

I live in the foothills of the Arizona desert, and quail frequently run up out of the wash behind our house and into our backyard. One morning, as Sande and I were having a cup of coffee, Mama and Papa Quail and several baby quail ran into the yard. The little ones darted all over the place as Mama Quail morphed into a sheepdog with feathers, trying to herd them into a clump to keep them together and safe.

Papa Quail? He didn't seem to be helping out much. In fact, he first looked like he was ignoring Mama and the babies. He flew up onto the birdbath, took a drink of water, and then sat there calmly, looking around.

Meanwhile, Mama was down there with the kids on her hands and knees, so to speak, looking a bit bedraggled. I wondered if she was feeling angry about her husband's lack of assistance, like most women on the planet would be (and rightfully so). Perhaps if Mama Quail could have squawked in English, she would have said to him, "You get off that birdbath, get down here, and give me a hand with these kids!"

But then I realized what Papa Quail was doing—exactly what he was supposed to. His role demanded that he seek higher ground so he could have that bird's-eye view to glimpse any coming danger to Mama Quail and those babies. That cat lurking in the bushes, looking for a light snack? One call from Papa and the babies ran immediately under the bushes, while he viciously besieged the cat from above until it slunk away, defeated and not likely to try anything with that same brood ever again.

As a male, Papa Quail was supposed to watch for any threats to his family, warn them if anything dangerous was headed their way, and give his all to protect his little brood.

I'm convinced that males everywhere—animal and human—have that same protective instinct. Their heartfelt desire is to protect the ones they love. When they can't or aren't allowed to play that role, they withdraw or shrink into themselves because they are unsure of their role. The smart woman learns not only to appreciate that natural drive of her husband but to use what she knows to both his advantage and hers to grow their relationship.

No marriage ever works—at least for long—if it's a superior-inferior relationship.

But men aren't off the hook either. There is a fine line between being protective and too protective or overbearing. Men and women are social equals in every way. No marriage ever works—at least for long—if it's a superior-inferior relationship.

You and your spouse are weak in some areas and strong in others. Those differences, when understood and appreciated, are what make your relationship satisfying and exciting.

38

Men and women are made to physically, mentally, and emotionally complement each other. However, the problem is that many—especially those in conservative circles—still struggle with how to handle societal changes of male and female roles and are unaware of how much such changes affect a marriage relationship. The resulting friction is like sandpaper between the two of you, rubbing each of you raw wherever you intersect.

#2: Marrying Too Early

Some couples struggle simply because they get married too early, before either husband or wife has the opportunity to realistically decide on a life direction. Like Alexis and Nate, for example. When they dated in high school, she wanted to be a nurse. He wanted to be a lawyer. But neither finished university because they were so "in love" and got married after their sophomore year.

Five years later, they have three kids. He directs kids' programs at a camp part-time and works part-time in a warehouse. She works part-time for an online company and cleans offices on the weekend. They juggle care for the kids. It's far from the romantic picture of a life together that either of them dreamed of.

When Alexis and Nate got married, loving each other was all that mattered. They didn't have any money apart from their parents, and they had no real job skills. Frankly, they had no idea how to cope with any of the problems life would throw at them. They really didn't know each other well except for their frequent wrestling matches in the back seat of the car or on her living room sofa when her parents weren't around.

Alexis and Nate thought marriage was like the Beatles' hit song "All You Need Is Love." But soon marriage was diapers, long work hours, pinching pennies, and lots of fighting—far different from the rose bouquets and sexual thrills they expected. They had never imagined nursing each other through a bout of the flu—complete with the prospect of mopping up vomit. Neither did they expect to pace the floor all night with a baby who had an ear infection.

"I wish someone would have told us how hard it would be," Nate confided to me. "Why didn't our parents stop us instead of shrugging and saying, 'Well, you'll do whatever you want to do'?" He was feeling trapped.

Whenever I encounter teens or college students who are determined to get married, I ask them a few simple questions:

- Do you like going to movie premieres and gaming online every Friday night? Are you prepared to give that up to get married?
- Do you like going out for dinner with friends? Are you prepared to stay home and eat PB&J instead or have them over for canned soup?
- Are you ready to start spending money on Pampers and formula instead of new clothes and iTunes downloads?
- Are you really that much in love that you can't wait to move in together?

Society is also greatly at fault. Parents today unwittingly push their teenagers into early dating. Just think about it. How many times did a well-intentioned aunt of yours ask, "So, is there anyone special in your life yet?" when you were only 15? Then you saw all those teen magazines that glorified makeup, the right hairstyle, and clothing to catch the guy of your dreams. Naturally, you started to assume that dating was something expected of you, and you were weird if you didn't do it.

How many times did a well-intentioned aunt of yours ask, "So, is there anyone special in your life yet?" when you were only 15?

Contrast that to a few years back, when I was a kid. In my elementary school, boys never could admit when they liked a girl. Even if that girl you liked brushed by you, you had to make a face and yell about getting cooties. That's how boys were expected to act.

Later in life, when you liked a girl, you hit her on the arm like you did a buddy. But things didn't work out like you expected. She cried, and you got in trouble for picking on a girl.

The girls? They chased you around the schoolyard not to kiss you but to give you a swift kick in the shins. That was the reigning battle of the sexes, and my own shins fell victim to it more than once.

Things have sure changed, haven't they?

Today, even young boys and girls feel pressure to date earlier, whether they're interested in the opposite sex or not. It's not unusual to see 13-year-olds holding hands or kissing. After all, they're bombarded with sexual images in the media that all have the same message: *If you want to be accepted by your peers and be top dog, you have to be desirable enough to have a boyfriend or girlfriend. Even more, you have to have sex. If you don't, there's something wrong with you.* That kind of peer pressure is tough because it's unrelenting.

Today's kids need to hear that it doesn't matter what anybody else says about you. What matters is that you are true to yourself, and that your actions line up with what you believe to be true about yourself.

However, many kids don't grow up with that message. Their home life is so miserable that any situation looks better than the one they're in at the moment. So grabbing at any offer of "love"— without thinking of consequences—is understandable.

Marty, 22, and Denise, 21, are a good example. Marty had been brought up in a permissive home where he was given far too many freedoms as a child and very few responsibilities. Denise grew up in a home where Mom and Dad had a very poor marriage. She met Marty when she was 14, when her parents were going through a rough divorce. To complicate the picture further, her father was an angry, abusive alcoholic.

Surrounded by messages of sex, the two quickly fell into a physically intimate relationship. But at 14 and 15, they weren't old enough to know the difference between love and infatuation. Lack of attention and love from her father drove Denise's involvement with Marty, who did pay attention to her. When she was 16, she dropped out of high school and they got married. She took a job as a cashier in a grocery store, and Marty got a job at a local carpentry factory. Somehow their marriage survived for five years, during which time they had a daughter.

But their relationship was clearly missing the love that should have connected them. Finally, it became evident that their union was destructive for each of them and for their daughter. They couldn't figure out why their lives were such a mess.

I could see why clearly. The pattern is similar to that of lots of couples who marry too early. They think they're falling in love, but their neediness has driven them into each other's arms.

Q: Why did Adam and Eve have a perfect marriage?
A: He didn't have to hear about all the men she could have married, and she didn't have to hear about the way his mother cooked.[1]

#3: Thinking That Living Together Is More Exciting Than Marriage

Hey, I'm a realist. I realize many people live together today, and no one even blinks an eye. Often couples tell me plainly, "We've been married for two years but living together for seven."

Sometimes when those couples tie the knot, their relationship starts to unravel. Disconnect follows because they don't know each other as well as they thought. Sure, they shared an apartment, dinner, and a bed, but such a living situation was temporary. Either of them could leave at a minute's notice. Now, with marriage, they feel a bit stuck, if they're honest.

If this is your situation, you're not alone. Many people who've lived together and then decided to get married have quietly told me, "Marriage isn't what I thought. It was a lot more exciting when we lived together." But that doesn't mean marriage *can't* be exciting. You *can* go after that intimate connection you've dreamed of, and I'll show you how. This section has important information you need to know up front to accomplish just that. So promise me—don't stop reading it, even if you might feel a wee little twinge here and there.

Testing the waters by living together to see if you're compatible is a bit like learning to play basketball by playing badminton. The two are completely unrelated. When you live together, you still think in terms of "mine" and "yours." You sometimes split the bills, or you vary who pays what bill. You have separate bank accounts. Then you get married and make the switch to "ours"—shared bank accounts, bills you pay together, etc.

> *Testing the waters by living together to see if you're compatible is a bit like learning to play basketball by playing badminton. The two are completely unrelated.*

Living together is such a common decision today that, according to *Psychology Today*, "more than 70% of US couples now cohabit before marriage."[2] But there's a hard fact you should know. Living together before you marry actually *increases* the probability of divorce. If you don't believe me, read it for yourself:

> Couples who lived together before they tied the knot saw a 33 percent higher rate of divorce than those who waited to live together until after they were married. Part of the problem was that cohabitors, studies suggested, "slid into" marriage without much consideration.[3]

Sharing the same four walls, bills, and the leftovers in the fridge may seem like a commitment, but it's more like a deluxe test that has fewer challenges (including permanency and children). If you want to stop the test, you just have to call a moving van. No court, no paperwork, no time to wait for a transition.

Though living together may feel like an intimate step, many studies found that "premarital cohabitation is associated with increased risk of divorce, a lower quality of marriage, poorer marital communication, and higher levels of domestic violence."[4] That's because many cohabiting couples never really take off their masks. They are still dating each other. That date may last a long time, but because there's no promised permanence, both partners try to keep their best foot forward.

So first there's love, then living together, then marriage . . . and often a baby carriage. After marriage, the couple relaxes enough to finally allow their masks to come off. That's when trouble comes, because both have established patterns based on those masks. The Prince Charming you thought you were living with—who buys you flowers, cooks you dinner, and rubs your back—turns back into the frog he really is, who doesn't shave or clean up after himself, much less think about doing sweet things for you.

Or the dazzling Cinderella you've been with 24-7 retreats back to scruffy Cinder-ella—since she no longer scrambles to get up before you so she looks good when you wake up. That same person who used to be so understanding when you were tired now relentlessly nags you to get a project done.

You argue about things that didn't use to matter. When he's late coming home from work, you wonder, *Who's he with?* But when you were living together, you saw other people without a problem.

Living together is a commitment, but it's a commitment not to make a full commitment.

In short, living together is a commitment, but it's a commitment *not* to make a full commitment.

Both men and women who have been in live-in situations tell me, "I feel cheated." They regret that they lived together instead of opting for a traditional marriage, because their ex-lovers have walked away. Not a single person has told me, "I'm glad we went for a trial run first, because it made us certain that we wanted to be married."

But research also shows that "the negative effects of cohabitation upon marriage are considerably reduced when the decision

44

to marry is taken before the couple cohabits."[5] Why did living together *after* getting engaged have different results? Because, researchers say, "the decision to get married takes place when the weight of cost, relative to love, was not bigger."[6] In other words, couples had *love* and a long-term future in mind as priorities, not simply saving on rent or utilities. Those who cohabit *before* they decide to get engaged because it's easier or cheaper often slide into marriage when kids arrive on the scene or the tax accountant tells them that married filing jointly would be a better option.

Combining any two people into a permanent relationship is always a challenge due to differing personalities, backgrounds, etc. It's more difficult when the two of you have played house for a few years without a commitment.

Is it possible for a couple who has lived together and then gets married to develop an intimate connection? Yes, of course. Despite where you started and where you've been, today is a new day. Your reality can match the dream of the marriage you desire.

Here are a few things you can do to ease the transition:

- Build up your trust by not hiding anything from your spouse. Let them know what you'll be doing, where, and with whom, and what time you're expected back. This isn't a "checking up on you" matter. It's a courtesy that married couples should naturally extend to each other.
- Change your "I" language to "we," and your thinking from "mine/his" or "mine/hers" to "ours." When you catch yourself saying, "I want . . . ," close your mouth and switch gears. Say instead, "Do you think it would be possible . . ."
- Don't be a bone digger. Keep the past in the past.
- Realize you'll have some oopses along the road. When those happen, forgive before the sun goes down. Get up fresh and start anew the next day.
- Set aside one evening for a date night every week. Do activities that will get you talking to each other on a deeper level.

(It's hard to talk just about the weather if you're facing each other naked in a hot tub.) Go for walks, share an ice cream cone, pretend like you're kids and play at the park. Just do it together, with cell phones off.

Even doing those five things will work wonders in your relationship.

Your spouse may or may not be ready to make a few changes in their behavior. Just remember, transformation starts with you and your willingness to make changes in yourself. That will be like catnip to your partner, irresistibly drawing them in to ponder, *What changed?*

That's when the fun action starts—the kind of one-upmanship game that's worth playing, since it'll win dividends for your relationship.

How to Undo Society's Damage on Your Relationship

TV shows about marriage often reveal dissatisfaction and failure. Men are comic buffoons who can't do anything right when it comes to their wives. Affairs and one-night stands, on the other hand, are portrayed as hot and passionate. In comparison, marriage can look pretty dull.

What's your image of married life? Does marriage indeed turn people into failures or dingbats, as sitcoms portray? Does it have to be dull? Is it impossible to find new topics to converse meaningfully about? Is it natural for time together to dim the passion and for you to be bored with each other?

Well, many married couples do live that sort of life. But it doesn't have to be that way. Yours doesn't have to be one of the high percentage of marriages that fizzles after seven years. You can develop and keep an intimate connection that stands the test of time.

The answer starts with a little information. Why are so many marriages in trouble? Why do husbands and wives feel disconnected? Why are they unable to communicate? If you're reading this book, it's because you are longing for more than you have—a different type of relationship.

Men, there's something you need to understand: women are relational at heart. They love to see how relationships play out, and that includes romantic ones. That little secret will help you understand why even females who are content in their marriage enjoy watching shows like *The Bachelor* or *The Bachelorette*. It's also why romantic novels and dramas are wildly popular—because they portray developing relationships (and yes, with a lot of romance thrown in).

Think of it this way. Women in general love shoes. They love looking for shoes even if they don't need them. I know because a while back I took my wife to Manhattan, New York. Of course she wanted to go shopping. And close to our hotel and Central Park, on 6th Avenue, was a slice of heaven. It's called Nine West, a shoe store. She was in that store for so long I thought she'd expired in the back room and perhaps no one had notified me. For *two hours* she looked at shoes and tried on shoes. Now, let me ask you, which of us men would do that?

But here's the kicker: she came out empty-handed. No shoes. Two hours and no shoes. Why? Because she simply loves looking at shoes and trying them on. And she had a great time doing it.

Sande wasn't done yet. We had to go down to Soho. There it took her just an hour. Then again, I'm used to waiting. This time she came out with two pairs of shoes. Trust me, she doesn't need shoes.

Okay, stop right there. Yes, I can hear some of you screaming at your book right now. "Leman, we *always* need shoes. We never have enough shoes."

But look at things from my perspective. I own only one pair of dress shoes. Just one. They're black loafers. I even bought them with tassels so I could wear them for all occasions. Otherwise I wear athletic shoes.

Then there's my wife.

Just like my wife enjoys looking at dozens of shoes, many women also enjoy shows like *The Bachelorette*, where the main character meets 14 or 15 guys. Then as they spend time together, talk about feelings, and share life, that woman goes through a lengthy process of elimination to decide which guy is really the one for her. The personalities and how they interact are fascinating studies in who gets along with whom and how, what problems develop, etc. It's no wonder relational shows like this have mesmerized such a large audience. Do men watch those shows? Sure! But largely the audience is women.

Men, you won't always understand your wife or everything she does. There are some things she will just do. Men tend to burp and spit even when they shouldn't. Women watch *The Bachelor* and *The Bachelorette* and love shopping for shoes even when they already have a closetful.

And for you naysayers, I understand. Not *every* woman likes to buy shoes or watch romance flicks, and not *every* man spits and grunts. But you've got to admit, many of them do.

So rest assured, gentlemen. When she watches those shows or reads those books, she's really not seeking another male to fall in love with. She's entertaining her relational side.

But don't forget that every woman is also still a girl at heart, dreaming of a little romance. How much better would it be if her romance partner was you?

Now *there's* a whole new reason to get to know your wife's needs and to bring her a red rose every once in a while.

SECRET #3

Preconceived Notions Matter

What your mom and dad did influences you far more than you know.

How many times have you told yourself, "I'll never say to my kids what my parents said to me"? But then you find yourself not only saying those very words but saying them with the same tone and even in a greater decibel than your parents did.

Or you said, "I hated the way my dad treated my mom. I'd never treat my wife like that." Then you treat your wife the same way. Flashes of your dad's anger and your mom's teary eyes are like a bad replay in your own marriage.

Or you think, *It doesn't really matter. I'll just do what raises the littlest fuss. What I want isn't important,* because you learned that staying under the radar at home was the best way to survive.

Why do you keep doing what you said you wouldn't do? And why do you see yourself the way you do? Largely because you learned it from your parents. If Mom and/or Dad didn't model a healthy family life—in the way they treated their kids and each other—how would you know what a good marriage should look like? You've never seen or experienced one. All you can do is model what you've seen as normal for male-female relationships.

Many adults today grew up with divorced or single parents, or one or more emotionally distant parents, along with a boatload of dating and sexual experimentation in the mix. With such a lack of role models, is it any wonder they're confused about what a healthy, mutually satisfying relationship should look like? Or that one or both partners has low self-worth?

What Role Models Really Teach You

Ron came to see me when his wife packed up their two boys and exited stage left. She said she couldn't trust him anymore and he was a bad role model for the boys.

"I just don't understand," he told me. "I've been a good husband. I bet I haven't had more than eight other women in the thirteen years we've been married."

Sad thing is, my jaw didn't drop, because that story was familiar. Girls and boys who grow up in an age of marital instability, infidelity, and divorce develop a negative view of relationships unless what goes on in their home counteracts what they see in society.

Girls and boys who grow up in an age of marital instability, infidelity, and divorce develop a negative view of relationships unless what goes on in their home counteracts what they see in society.

Ron's dad himself had so many extramarital affairs that Ron thought he was being a good husband and father by limiting himself to less than one affair per year. And what about his two boys? As almost adolescents, what were they learning about the way men should treat women from watching their father?

Interestingly, Ron's father's boyhood idol was John F. Kennedy, who treated women as sexual playthings (something JFK learned from his own father). Ron's father had

PARENT ALERT

Kids really do model what they see. I got a firsthand reminder of that truth when I was driving down a city street with my son, Kevin II, who was two years old. Suddenly I got an urge to, of all gross things, spit. No sooner had I rolled up the window, though, when I caught a big one on the side of my neck from my son. Little Kevin had perfectly modeled his daddy's behavior, much to my own chagrin—especially when I caught an earful from Mrs. Uppington, my beloved and proper wife, who didn't appreciate such role-modeling.

That day I learned more than "be careful where and when you spit." It was a good reminder that I better practice everything I preach because little eyes are always watching.

passed that philosophy on to his son, who was now reaping the harvest of two generations of philandering . . . and perhaps more, if Ron had known any history on his grandfather.

Ron, though, to his credit, came to see me because he wanted to know how to turn things around. He truly loved his wife and kids. He wanted to stay in their lives and do things right. He just wasn't sure what "right" was, or how to go about it. Without role models in his life of what a healthy marriage should look like, he needed lots of coaching.

The good news is that Ron stepped up to the plate as a husband and father. He did the long, hard work not only to change his own perspective and habits but also to win his wife's love and trust all over again. He didn't want to pass the broken baton of his own upbringing to his two boys. I was honored to be at his and his wife's recommitment ceremony several years later.

When a little boy grows up in a home where his father treats his mother like trash, chances are that without intervention, he'll grow up to treat his own wife like trash. If a little girl sees her mother running around on her father or making him look stupid in front of others, she'll come to think of her own sexuality in terms of using, emasculating, and conquering men.

Because of inadequate role modeling, many men and women fall into using each other instead of putting the work into building an intimate, lifetime connection.

Women use men as providers, as escorts, and as disciplinarians when they don't want to lower the boom on the kids themselves. How many times have you heard a woman say to a child, "Just you wait until your father gets home"? And she delivers a threat that makes the child stop doing whatever naughty or annoying thing they're doing.

Men use women to boost their own egos, making them feel like nothing more than objects on display or, worse, sexual receptacles.

Annie was a good example of that kind of fallout. She'd been married for five years. "I'm so tired," she told me. "Tired of being used." She said the only interaction she really had with her husband after marriage was when he felt like having sex. She was tired of feeling like an object but didn't know how to be anything else.

Like her mother, Annie was beautiful. Both women had fallen early for older guys who gave them attention and treated them like pheasants under glass while they were dating. Then after "I do," the tables turned quickly. Sadly, she'd learned that being obedient and doing whatever her husband wanted her to do was the only way to maintain the fragile peace in her house. After all, she'd seen that type of relationship play out between her parents.

Annie had grown up in a home where her dad called the shots. She was never allowed to have an opinion or make any of her own decisions. Because she went straight from home to a conservative college and married as soon as she graduated, she had no opportunity to experience life on her own. Her husband, Brad, had grown up as the favored child in his household and got all he wanted and more. As an adult, he was a clone of her dad—controlling, calling every shot.

Their marriage "worked" for a while because both continued their childhood patterns. But when Annie's friends questioned the way her husband treated her, she began to wonder, *Why does it always have to be his way? Don't I matter?* It was the first time she'd ever thought of herself as a person who should have the right to make decisions. Confusion, resentment, and then quiet rebellion grew and took more than two years to come to a head.

The resulting explosion stunned Brad, who at first thought his wife had suddenly morphed into an alien creature. Like with Ron, Brad's view of male-female roles was long entrenched from watching his parents.

Both Annie and Brad needed some reeducation about their own life mantras and how those philosophies impacted each of them and their relationship. They also needed to know what healthy interaction between men and women should be like before they could begin to move toward an intimate connection that could last a lifetime.

A lack of healthy parental role models can do deep relational damage to the next generation. If a girl's mom teaches her she's only acceptable as a woman if she's a homemaker and subservient to men, she will tend to pursue that path—even if she wants to become a doctor or lawyer. That's because she's developed a life mantra: *I'm only acceptable if I do those things.* She limits her own potential because of what she believes about herself.

If a young boy never sees a caring, loving father who meets the needs of his wife and children on a daily basis, but rather sees his dad continually dump on his mom, then he'll determine that women are for using and will select a marriage partner he thinks he can use.

The Roots of Self-Worth

If you have a healthy self-worth, you will seek out someone who treats you well, and you won't put up with ill treatment. If you struggle with self-worth, you will tend to date or marry partners who reinforce the negative image of yourself. Sure, in the beginning the romance may have colored your view a bit. However, once that romance wore off, the treatment you received was what you expected—likely because it's what you received growing up.

Mary is just one of the many women I've counseled who went from being verbally abused by her father to being verbally abused by her husband. The guy she married treated her the way she thought she deserved to be treated. He was just like dear ol' Dad . . . who wasn't so dear. She was overly submissive and compliant. Their marriage was far from a partnership between equals. It was more like she jumped to do his bidding the instant he called.

By contrast, Allie—who grew up in a home that was similar to Mary's—married a man who literally swept her off her feet and treated her like a princess. However, after three years of marriage, they struggled to communicate.

"I can't tell her anything. She gets so defensive the minute I make any suggestion at all," her husband confided to me. Her low self-worth had prompted her to be defensive. She viewed even innocent words and actions as insults and criticisms of her as a person. Because she thought she deserved to be put down, any statement her husband made was immediately perceived as negative.

Allan was reared in a home where his dad ruled the roost. The minute his dad arrived home, Allan escaped to his room. If he wasn't in the vicinity, he figured, he wasn't in firing range of his dad's comments about how he'd never amount to anything. His mom, meanwhile, felt bad for Allan and smoothed her son's path in nearly everything behind the scenes—even hiding his report cards from her husband.

Years later, Allan had fulfilled his dad's prophecy of not amounting to anything, other than getting married and having a couple of kids. He hadn't gone to college, had gotten a low-end job, and plodded through his days until he could return home to his easy chair and computer game.

His wife was exhausted and fed up. "How can you make somebody care?" she pleaded with me. "He doesn't seem to care about anything."

The answer is, you can never *make* anybody care. Caring is an individual choice. Allan was a classic case of a firstborn perfectionist who saw himself as a failure because his perfectionistic, controlling father saw him that way. He'd lost his passion to pursue anything because he'd given up trying to do and be anything for fear of disappointing his father. He was living in "hold" mode.

Anytime damaged self-worth enters the picture, your relationship will only get worse unless you choose to deal with the root of the low self-worth head-on. Why does one or both of you feel negative about yourself? How is that prompting you to view each other? Marriage only works long-term if both of you are equal, respected partners.

Marriage only works long-term if both of you are equal, respected partners.

Learned Behavior

I once saw a video where a monkey was taken out of its cage at a zoo and turned loose to play in a nearby pasture. Every couple of feet that monkey would thrust his body forward as if attempting to jump from bar to bar, even though there were no bars.

What was that monkey demonstrating? Learned behavior he'd incorporated over the past 15 years of captivity. That behavior was such a part of the monkey's life that it was difficult for him to process his environment any other way. Changing his environment didn't change his personality or behavior. He was still the same monkey.

We humans are very much like that monkey. No, I'm not talking Darwinism. I'm saying that just because we grow up, it doesn't mean we will change unless we choose to. Behaviors and life mantras learned from our childhood relationships and experiences follow us into adulthood.

Just because we grow up, it doesn't mean we will change unless we choose to. Behaviors and life mantras learned from our childhood relationships and experiences follow us into adulthood.

Everything your parents did and didn't do affected you. In the same way, everything you do and don't do affects your spouse and any kids you have.

If you've learned somewhere along the way that marriage is like a prison sentence, that sex is something shameful, that extramarital affairs or one-night stands are no big deal, all of those will influence your own marriage relationship. But no matter where your relationship is now, I guarantee that you can grow closer as you come to understand how inadequate role models have impacted you.

Half Circle or Whole Circle?

Positive change in your relationship always starts with you. If you choose to do some things differently, your spouse has more reason to do things differently too. Marriage is the joining of two people, but you have to be comfortable with yourself before you can be comfortable with revealing your true self to another person.

As one smart woman I know said, "A half circle and a half circle can't become a whole circle in marriage. The best marriage is when two already whole circles—people with healthy self-worth and relational patterns—choose to overlap each other." She even posted a simple math equation on the fridge as a daily reminder to her dating teenagers:

So if you're not healthy, start with yourself.[1] Healthy people have a realistic view of themselves and their place in the universe.

They're not king or queen, but neither are they pawns with no control over their actions or future.

There's no such thing as a perfect human being. Everyone makes mistakes. But if you're healthy, you can say those critical words when you do something wrong: "I'm sorry I hurt you. Please forgive me. I will do better."

Then you choose to act differently from that point forward.

BONUS SECTION

Be Your Own Counselor

Picture the following situations and then ask yourself what you would do.

Scenario 1: Your spouse arrives home after a busy day to find you already home from work and partway through dinner preparations. He comes up behind you and gives you a loving back hug.
What I would do:

Scenario 2: You know your spouse has had a wild week and has a lot to accomplish before holiday visitors arrive. You hear a wild clattering and upset exclamations in the kitchen and run in to see what's happening. The soup that was supposed to be for dinner has boiled over on the stove.
What I would do:

Scenario 3: You come around the corner and get hit by a flying underwear missile. Your spouse has attempted to carry the laundry basket, stacked too high, down the stairs and it has dumped over, scattering your unmentionables like a rain shower.
What I would do:

Now let's replay those scenarios with both a typical reaction and a creative response.

Scenario 1: Your spouse arrives home after a busy day to find you already home from work and partway through dinner preparations. He comes up behind you and gives you a loving back hug.

> **Reaction 1:** You yank loose from the embrace, swivel, and pin him with a glare that communicates, *Do you mind? I'm busy, and the children are watching!*

Response 2: You turn off the burner, swivel in his arms, and plant a warm welcome-home kiss on his lips, right there in front of the two cherubs.

Scenario 2: You know your spouse has had a wild week and has a lot to accomplish before holiday visitors arrive. You hear a wild clattering and upset exclamations in the kitchen and run in to see what's happening. The soup that was supposed to be for dinner has boiled over on the stove.

Reaction 1: "What's wrong with you?" you exclaim. "It's just soup. Can't you do anything right?"

Response 2: You stop in the doorway to assess the situation and your overwhelmed spouse. You step in, turn off the burner, and say calmly, "Honey, why don't you go change clothes and relax a little? Maybe even take a shower to wash this rough week off. I'll clean this up. Don't worry about dinner. I'll take care of it."

Scenario 3: You come around the corner and get hit by a flying underwear missile. Your spouse has attempted to carry the laundry basket, stacked too high, down the stairs and it has dumped over, scattering your unmentionables like a rain shower.

Reaction 1: You stop dead in your tracks and pluck the underwear off your head. Your steely glare and "I can't believe you're such an idiot" head shake says it all before you walk away.

Response 2: You stop dead in your tracks and pluck the underwear off your head. You start laughing. "Well, this is just too funny." You start scooping up scattered and dirty unmentionables. "Wow, that's a big load. The next time you have so much, let me know, and I'd be happy to help you carry some down and get a load started. After all, it's my underwear too."

What's the difference between the endings to those scenarios? *Reactions* are always given without thinking. They naturally follow patterns you've seen and experienced. *Responses* are chosen, with the other person and your long-term future together in mind.

Think of it this way. When doctors say you've *reacted* to medicine, that's bad. If they say you're *responding* to medicine, that's good. It's the same in relationships.

In Scenario 1, you're likely to *react* in such a way if you grew up in a home where there was little loving expression between your parents and where anything considered remotely intimate was for the bedroom only—definitely not in front of the children. But by reacting this way, you'll pass that same unhealthy attitude about intimacy on to your kids—that it's not okay for couples to hug and kiss.

However, if you set aside what you would instinctively do—withdraw from any embrace—and think about growing your long-term connection with your spouse, you'll accept his expression of love. You'll also go farther to show how happy you are to see him. When you do so, you promote a win-win marriage for both of you and role-model a healthy relationship for your kids that will pay dividends in their future.

Those kids will learn that it's not only okay but it's normal for a husband and wife to treat each other with tenderness and affection. Yes, those kids may say, "Eww, Mom and Dad are kissing! Gross!" and run away, squealing like piggies down the hallway. But inside, they're thinking, *Mom and Dad are good. They're happy too. They'll stay together.* Such displays give your kids security and stability in a tumultuous world of broken and changing relationships.

In Scenario 2, such a reaction is selfishly based on thinking only about yourself, your own needs, and how tough you have it at work. It's a typical one made by men who believe a woman's place is in the kitchen and that her work isn't all that hard—even though she does basically everything for him behind the scenes.

However, those who acknowledge their spouse's hard work, that they have extra to-dos on their mind right now, and that they just need a break to get on an even keel—those spouses are worth more than their weight in gold. They'll lovingly go out of their way to provide that break—even if it means ordering Chinese takeout for the second night in a row because it's her favorite stress food.

In Scenario 3, such a reaction is very disrespectful. If you have the guts—and stupidity—to do or say something like that to anyone, clearly you don't appreciate their work. If I were them, I'd dump the rest of that dirty laundry basket over your head, walk out the door, and go have a nice dinner by myself somewhere while you do the laundry. No one deserves to be treated like that.

But if you lighten up and find the humor in the goofy things that happen, your shared laughter will bring a closer connection. So will flexing your muscles and taking time to help the one you love.

See the difference between reacting and responding? When you react, you don't give yourself time to think before old instincts—those patterned by your parents and the home you grew up in—kick in. When you respond, you pause for 10 seconds while you think, *What did I use to do? That didn't work, right? It only fuels the fight, so I don't want to do it again. I refuse to behave like my parents did. So what should I do now that would be different and good for our relationship long-term?*

Those seconds will be worth it. Trust me.

SECRET #4

There's No Reason to Settle for Blah, Less-Than, or a Battlefield

The top four reasons couples feel disconnected . . . and what you can do about it.

Let me ask you a key question: Does your relationship right now match the dream you had in your head when you decided this was the man or woman you wanted to spend a lifetime with?

If you admitted, "No," that doesn't make you a bad person. You simply joined the ranks of all the honest readers of this book. And congratulations are in order because you've plucked up your courage to go after the intimate connection you desire, instead of settling for blah, less-than, or a battlefield in your marriage.

Why do couples start to feel disconnected? Here are the four main reasons.

Reason #1: "The Romance Has Died"

Your husband used to bring you flowers and call you on his work break just because he wanted to hear your voice. He used to hang on your every word when you were dating. He even drove by your work and tucked a love note under the windshield wiper of your car.

Now you can't remember the last time you got flowers, a call, or a love note, and he seems to tune you out the instant you open your mouth.

When you were dating, your girlfriend showed up at your soccer game with brownies for you and the guys. Because you're an avid sports fan, she enjoyed a bowl of popcorn with you during Monday night football and even asked what some of the terms meant. She watched a few soccer matches and tennis games and seemed interested in learning some of the nuances of the games.

Now that you're married, she rolls her eyes at you as soon as you put up your feet in front of the tube. She thinks it's stupid to spend time watching a bunch of grown men running around kicking a leather ball and trying to knock each other down, and she doesn't hesitate to let you know you could spend your time better elsewhere—like getting the car washed.

What happened? Why has the romance disappeared?

Both of you have put the desire to please each other on the back burner. Men are wired to compete. During dating, he pulled out all the stops to show you how much he cared about you to secure his prize. Now that you're married, he has turned his focus to other things.

You, too, have multiple things tugging at you—work, your parents or in-laws, kids, friends, grocery shopping, and other real-life issues. When you were dating, you would lie awake at night, dreaming up fun little things to do to show that guy he was special and needed in your life. Now you're so tired that as soon as your head hits the pillow, the only thing on your mind is sleep, and within seconds you're out cold.

If your marriage is lacking romance, now's a good time to ask yourself, *What have I done lately to show my spouse I appreciate her/him?* It doesn't take big things like a diamond, a Caribbean cruise, or a full-blown romantic weekend at an expensive hotel to please your spouse. Small demonstrations of love and appreciation go a long way toward making up the deficit of romance in your marriage.

Think back a bit. What little things did you do when you were dating that meant a lot to each other? Why not do even one of those today? Why not focus on pleasing your spouse like you used to? No, your spouse likely isn't treating you the same way either. But if you want your marriage to change, you have to start with you.

In relationships you generally receive back what you give. If you give anger, you'll receive anger. If you give resentment, you'll receive resentment. If you give kindness, you'll receive kindness. If you do small caring acts, you'll receive small caring acts. Yes, it may take time to restore your marriage, especially if you've both lived in Antarctica for a while, but the sooner you start, the sooner your spouse can respond likewise. If you try to please your spouse, they may at first be surprised, but it will likely spark them wanting to please you too.

In relationships you generally receive back what you give.

Reason #2: "I Thought I Could Change Him/Her"

Many people enter marriage thinking they can change each other if they just work hard enough.

> "I know he's a little laid-back now, but if we have kids, his drive to work will kick in."

> "She's a terrible cook, but if I get my mom to show her, she'll eventually be as good as my mom."

> "He's bad with money because he's always had enough. I'm sure he'll learn how to manage it, though, if we get a mortgage."

> "She's super messy and I'm a neatnik, but I'm sure she'll fall into line when we get a place together."

I always tell dating couples, "Never go into marriage with the thought of changing each other. If you can't love and accept each other exactly as you are—strengths and weaknesses—don't get married."

If you're already married, though, you need to accept your spouse, warts and all. After all, you *chose* that person, didn't you? Nagging, putting each other down, pouting, or any other negative methods only garner anger and resentment and will drive you farther apart. An old proverb says, "You catch more flies with honey than with vinegar." The same is true of human beings.

Mark and Aileen were drawn toward each other because they were complete opposites, as often happens. Mark, an accountant, was all about precision, timing, and doing things by the book. Aileen, a photographer, was spontaneous, emotional, and an out-of-the-box thinker. It doesn't take a rocket scientist to realize the clashes that occurred in nearly every aspect of their marriage—from choosing their first apartment to juggling finances and schedules.

An old proverb says, "You catch more flies with honey than with vinegar." The same is true of human beings.

Their marriage was hit harder when Aileen became pregnant right after she'd started her first official job. When I met the two, they had been married for four years, had a toddler, and exchanged several barbs within the first few minutes in my office.

"She's never on time, and it drives me absolutely crazy," he said. "It's a big problem."

"All he thinks about is what we have to do when. He can never enjoy anything," she fired back. "He just has to get to the next activity. With him, it's only schedule, schedule, schedule. Never me. Never his son."

It had never crossed their minds that instead of trying to change each other, they needed to enjoy each other's strengths, shore up each other's weaknesses, and extend some grace to a fellow human being.

She needed to understand why he was so scheduled—because he'd been raised with two perfectionistic parents who frowned at his slightest mistakes. He feared failure, so he kept a tight rein on everything he did in life.

He needed to understand that she'd been reared by a dad who was emotionally distant and busy in his job—just like Mark was becoming—and by a mom who was rarely home and didn't provide boundaries either. Having someone calling the shots on her life now was suffocating.

Let me ask you this: What first drew the two of you together? Likely it was your differences that brought the sparks that made you pursue each other. But those same differences can tear you apart after marriage, if you decide that your spouse has to be like you and you try to change him or her.

What first drew the two of you together? Likely it was your differences that brought the sparks that made you pursue each other.

But if you try thinking of those differences another way and come to understand them, you'll spark an intimate, growing connection. That connection will help you flex during situations where you'd normally be irritated and will allow you to see even humor in your differences.

Reason #3: "We Don't Talk Anymore"

Think back to when you were dating. You couldn't wait to talk to the person you were falling in love with. You craved more time together and wanted to know all about them. You texted like a mad woodpecker, FaceTimed when you were away from each other, and shared long conversations over the phone and over dinner.

Fast-forward to now. Some of you barely talk except the occasional grunt of acknowledgment or to ask who's getting the groceries for the week. When you do talk, neither of you walk away happy.

Do any of the following sound familiar?

- Your spouse's eyes glaze over when you talk for more than a minute about a subject. When you say, "Are you listening to me? Why aren't you saying anything?" he fires back, "Of course I hear you. How can I not? You talk and talk but never say anything important that's worth responding to."
- You try to explain what's bothering you, but your spouse jumps in before you can finish with his own complaint: "That bothers you? Really? Well, *you* . . ."
- You try to point out one of your spouse's weaknesses and she gets upset, even when you're offering "constructive" criticism.
- Your spouse is the king of words like *always* and *never*: "You *always* drag my mother into this." "You *never* take my feelings into consideration."
- Your spouse assumes—wrongly—that she always knows what's going on in your head.
- Your partner monopolizes the conversation so you never get to share your thoughts.
- Your spouse blames you for everything and never accepts her share for what happens.
- He's got a great memory for what you did wrong five years ago, and he keeps bringing it up.
- She's masterful at passing the buck of blame.

If you're wincing because some of these hit home, you two have fallen into negative communication patterns.

Assuming what's going on in your spouse's mind is never a good idea. Neither is asking a question such as, "Why won't you tell me what you're thinking or feeling?" or demanding, "Tell me what you're thinking!" It's much better to say in a straightforward, unemotional manner, "I'd really like to know what you're thinking and feeling. That's important to me."

Words like *always* and *never* trap your loved one because they overstate any case and up the ante on any disagreement. Many times those two words fly out when you assume you know what your spouse is thinking. But such words are partners that go along with accusing your spouse of wrong motives.

Do you really know what's going on in their mind? Then don't assume negatively. Avoid statements like, "You always do this to make me feel bad. Then you know I'll give in," and, "You'll never learn. I might as well give up trying." If you say these, you'll be defeated before you start, because your spouse—especially if he's male—has already tuned you out.

Assuming what's going on in your spouse's mind is never a good idea.

When playing the blame game, nobody ever wins. As soon as you try to assess blame, both of you lose. In marriage, there are no winners and no losers. Either you both win or you both lose. So when things go wrong in your relationship, you need to be willing to share the responsibility.

Easier said than done, I know. Part of the blame game involves digging up history—like the dog digging up his bone from two years ago and dragging it onto your porch. Don't go there. Instead, focus on the present and look for positive solutions.

No matter what your current communication patterns are, you can change them. These few powerful words are a good start: "I'm sorry." "I was wrong." "Please forgive me."

Yes, they take swallowing some pride and stepping past any resentment or anger. But isn't your marriage worth it? And aren't you reading this book because you want to see changes in your relationship?

Reason #4: "We Never See Each Other"

With the married-singles lifestyle becoming more and more common—the "I do my thing and she does hers" philosophy—each

UNDERSTANDING MALES 101

Ladies, here are a few secrets you need to know about us as males.

Secret #1: *We tune out if any description is too long, too vague, or too emotional.* If you want a male to respond to any subject, be direct. Use short sentences and go for one point rather than multiple ones. We guys get sidetracked easily. If you don't stick to one point in attempting to solve a problem, for example, and you jump from topic to topic, you lose or bamboozle us. We're not stupid, just simple.

Secret #2: *We're intimidated by your mastery of words.* Women are so much better at talking than men. Because you're innately programmed to use three and a half times the amount of words men do, it's easy to monopolize a conversation. However, if you're too busy talking, we guys don't have a chance to say anything. By the time we've formed our thoughts into words, you've already jumped the gun on the next topic.

Or, even worse, we hear the dreaded "Are you listening to me?" harangue because you assume we're simply not listening. Really, we are. Our male brains just take longer to process before we can speak. And remember, we can only handle one request or complaint at a time. If you give us a flood of them, we're paralyzed because we aren't sure which one we should address first. After all, one of our greatest skills as guys is thinking through all angles of a single issue at a time.

Secret #3: *We're terrified of your tears.* Guys in general are scared of girls crying, especially the women we love—our wives and daughters. When too much emotion is racing around, we males shut down.

It's like the newlywed husband who saw his wife crying in the kitchen. Hands raised in helplessness, he said, "Uh, I'll come back later," and backed out of the kitchen.

She was stupefied. She was only crying because she was cutting onions, not because she was upset about something.

But because he saw his beloved bride crying, that tough guy, who'd specialized in wrestling in high school, didn't know what to do. He didn't have sisters, and he'd never seen his mom cry, because she did so behind closed doors, in private. The concept was so new and terrifying to him that he simply shut down. He didn't have time to assess the entire situation. He didn't see the cutting board and onions. He simply saw his wife crying and fled.

Yup, that's us guys, unless we've been trained by our mamas to respond differently. So don't hold it against us. Just gently educate us about what you'd like us to do, and we'll gladly follow through.

Think of us a little bit like trained seals. Throw us a fish and we'll do anything for you.

---

spouse has their own job, eats dinner on the fly separately, and spends their downtime differently.

Max and Sherry are a good example. Max spends his weekends fishing or hunting with his buddies, plays games every Thursday night, and bowls in a league a couple of nights a week. Sherry works out at the gym two nights after work and spends her weekends with her girlfriends, shopping, going out for dinner, and watching movies. The only times the two interact are when they need more laundry detergent or happen to share some couch time for a favorite TV show.

When I want to know how a couple is doing, I ask how they spend their time. That's a good indication of what priorities are important to them. Whenever I see couples who don't spend time together, I always wonder why they got married in the first place—unless it was merely to have cheaper rent. If you love someone, you *want* to spend time with them. That person becomes a top priority.

> *When I want to know how a couple is doing, I ask how they spend their time. That's a good indication of what priorities are important to them.*

But for many couples, the label *marriage* simply means, "Well, we're married now, so see you later," and they go about their lives.

Should couples spend *all* their time together? No, that's not healthy either. In fact, it's unrealistic and can become suffocating.

Love doesn't demand its own way. It simply puts the other as a top priority.

Spending time with friends is important, as well as growing your own hobbies. There's nothing wrong with a man spending a weekend in Colorado to mountain bike with his friends, or a woman having a three-day vacation with girlfriends at Lake Tahoe. But if you're married, your spouse should be your top life priority, and that means spending most of your free time together. If you aren't growing together, you're growing apart.

"But Dr. Leman," you say, "you don't understand. Our schedules are so busy with work, the kids, all the things we're involved in. . . ."

Stop right there. Take a look at that schedule. How you spend your time reveals what your priorities really are. Do you really need to be on that committee that meets every Wednesday night? Do you have to take that extra work project? Do your kids need to be involved in every activity they are?

You'd be amazed how getting out the scissors and trimming that crazy schedule will not only bring you relief but also allow you to find time for each other. Isn't your marriage worth that kind of consideration?

SIMPLE WAYS TO SAY "I LOVE YOU"

- Every night or morning, tell your spouse one thing you appreciate about them.
- Provide a little reminder every week to say, "I love you and I'd still choose you all over again." Maybe it's a note written on top of take-out coffee, a balloon tied to your mailbox to welcome her home, a single flower on her pillow, a handmade card tucked into a briefcase for a work trip. . . . Use your imagination.
- Be creative in finding ways to spend time together that your spouse will enjoy. Perhaps it's planting flower seeds in a window box, a book to read and discuss, or a new gourmet recipe to try.

I strongly believe that every couple, to be and stay healthy, should spend at least one night a week doing something alone together. That means just the two of you, minus any kids or any other human appendages like friends or relatives. It could be a movie, taking a walk in the park, or dinner out somewhere (or even better, send the kids to Grandma's and you stay in with a candlelit evening of your own). Whatever you do, that night should involve an activity that both of you enjoy. If one of you has a revolving work schedule, make sure to choose a day at the beginning of every week that you both can anticipate and then stick to it. Your time together is far more important than anything else that might come up.

Everyday reality hardly ever matches the dream . . . unless you work together on becoming one as husband and wife. Whether you've been married for a few months or many years, there is something you can learn about creating an ongoing romance, adjusting to changes in each other, learning how to communicate more effectively, and spending time together.

You've already invested significant time in your greatest treasure— the spouse you chose. So don't stop there. You two deserve the marriage of your dreams. Why not give it your all to get exactly what you desire?

SECRET #5

Yup, Men and Women
Are Different

Exploring your spouse's needs and how you
can best meet them.

Can you honestly say that you always understand your spouse?

Me neither. Life sure would be simpler if we did, huh?

Then again, it would probably be a lot more boring.

Men and women couldn't be more different. Unless you slept through sex ed class in middle school or have lived solo on a desert island, you can't miss the obvious differences. We have different bodies with different chemistries, different minds with different personalities, and different characteristics and different needs.

When women traipse off to the ladies' room, they have to go *together*, like a covey of quail—in groups of two, eight, twelve, or fourteen. They even ask other females to go with them.

I doubt there's a man on the planet who has even considered that possibility. If there's one thing I prefer to do by myself, behind a door that's bolted in four places, it's going potty.

A man can drive through three counties, completely lost, and never ask for directions. Females? They'll ask for directions from the shoe department to the dress department in Dillard's.

Females are also masters at giving directions to the dentist's office such as, "You can't miss it. There are some beautiful flower beds right in front of the office. But don't go in the front door. That looks like his office but it's not. Go in the side entrance."

A man can drive through three counties, completely lost, and never ask for directions. Females? They'll ask for directions from the shoe department to the dress department in Dillard's.

That's my Sande, and those are the exact directions she gave me when I had to take one of our kids to the dentist. The street name, address, nearby roads that intersected—none of that seemingly was important. I could go driving all day around Tucson, looking for those "beautiful flower beds" right in front of a front door that's not the entrance, and never find them.

Sande, to her credit, had such a lovely memory of the front of the dentist's office, and she was concerned that I go in the right doorway. That's all very nice, but I'm a guy. I need coordinates on the map. Give me an address and I'll hunt that puppy down. I'll bag it and put a bow around it. Just provide me with the specifics and I'm on it. I likely won't notice the flowers, but I'll get the job done. That kid will get to the dentist right on time.

Then again, if she gave those same directions to a girlfriend, that friend would nod and say, "Oh, I know exactly where you mean. Those flowers *are* beautiful, aren't they? Did you know . . . ?"

Then the two would be off in a barrage of descriptive words that would leave me speechless, with merely a raised eyebrow for a response. After having a wife and four daughters, I've long ago given up following the flurry of words between females, except for when I hear, "Leemie, are you paying attention?" Then my brain snaps into gear.

Sande's description and my response highlight one of the many differences that occur in the way husbands and wives think.

Variety—the Spice of Any Marriage

My beloved bride and I are also different in a lot of other ways.

She's a five-forker—the kind of woman who loves those restaurants that give you five forks. I prefer one fork, and if it's plastic, all the better. I can even do without the fork if the situation calls for it. My idea of fine eating establishments is the Waffle House.

Sande delights in giving her friends presents wrapped with ribbon and sprinkled with aromatic potpourri. Doing such a thing has never entered my brain. Neither does learning the right kind and color of potpourri for the occasion.

She loves to get her hair and nails done, making a daylong excursion out of it with a little lunch in between with friends. I prefer to do my nails at a red light with my front teeth in 10 seconds or less. As far as my hair goes, a baseball cap works nicely . . . until Sande insists I get my hair cut.

Sande likes "sharing." I like three-word sentences.

Clearly men and women are different. That's what drew you to each other in the first place and caused the tinglies that made you notice each other across the crowd. After all, what fun would it be just hanging out with someone exactly like yourself all the time? Or talking to yourself?

However, let me be clear on something I feel strongly about. In today's push for gender equality, we often confuse equality with sameness. But men and women are not the same. It's like saying an aardvark and an armadillo are the same critters. No, they're different animals.

In today's push for gender equality, we often confuse equality with sameness.

Are the sexes equal? Absolutely. But, I repeat, *they are not the same.*

FOR
WOMEN ONLY

You're simply amazing to us guys. You're the emotional one who colors our world with fun and organizes us, and the wordsmith who paves the way for us to talk and share our heart. You're the relational expert who can make a new friend simply by meeting her in the restroom at an event.

We want to please you, but sometimes we really don't know how to do that. We need your help . . . but gently. Inside this grown-up body is a little boy's tender heart that can get squished easily. So give us some grace and treat us with TLC. We may not always look like we're trying, but we are, because you mean more to us than anyone on the planet. We just don't know how to tell you that.

Being a woman doesn't mean you have to grow your hair long and like to wear skirts. Neither does being a male mean you have to like hunting, fishing, and playing lumberjack on the weekends. Such categorization is simplifying, suffocating, and simply untrue. We all have differing personalities, gifts, and interests.

Even men's and women's brains are wired differently. We can look at the exact same stimuli and different parts of our brains will light up. That's because men and women tend to interpret the same situations differently. No wonder there's friction sometimes. That's why I say that God Almighty was the original humorist when he created two beings so completely different and then said, "The two shall become one." I'm sure he had some good laughs over Adam's and Eve's initial interactions with each other.

However, a healthy and happy marriage is one in which both partners understand, accept, and celebrate those differences—and learn how to relate to each other even though they see the world very differently.

The Secret of a Successful Marriage

As a marriage counselor and psychologist for umpteen years, I've been asked frequently, "What's the number-one secret for a successful marriage?"

My response is, hands down, "Become an expert in meeting your spouse's needs. Then they'll never be tempted to look elsewhere."

The majority of affairs occur because one of the partners feels ignored, belittled, or left in the dust by the other. In a world of hefty divorce rates, want to divorce-proof your marriage? Then pay attention to your spouse and meet their needs.

Will you be able to meet all of those needs? No, because you're human. You'll never bat 1,000. But you at least have to get that bat off your shoulder and give it your best swing for a home run.

In order to meet those needs, you first have to know what they are. Thinking your spouse's needs are just like yours is not only an incorrect assumption but a deadly one.

Take Ralph and Angie, for instance. When they got married, he assumed that she wanted what he did—a really nice roof over her head, matching furniture, the latest flat-screen TV, and an occasional vacation cruise—so he worked hard and even put in overtime hours to provide those things for her.

But what did Angie want? Long moonlit walks, fireside chats, hugs, simple vacations with s'mores over a campfire, and three kids to share life's adventures with. After all, he seemed to love that stuff when they were dating.

Fast-forward seven years. He's sprawled out in front of that flat-screen TV, watching the Green Bay Packers play the Chicago Bears, and she's perched on that matching chair wanting to talk about their relationship.

What's her problem? What's his problem? Both of them will be confused and resentful until they realize something critically important. The problem isn't each of them individually; it's where they interact as a couple. His needs and her needs are very different.

Until both partners realize that, they won't be able to develop an intimate connection, talk about it, and learn how to meet each other's needs to the best of their abilities.

Whether you've been married for a few months, a few years, or decades, to craft a healthy, mutually satisfying relationship, you have to view life through your spouse's eyes. That means you first must understand the top three needs of men and the top three needs of women.

What a Man Needs

Compared to complex women, we men are simple creatures. Here are our top three needs, starting with the most important.

To Be Needed

A while back, there was a saying: "A woman needs a man like a fish needs a bicycle."

But that's completely wrong. To have an intimate connection, the saying should be, "Wives need husbands like fish need water, and husbands need wives the same way."

Some women bristle at the very suggestion that they need a man. However, marriage isn't a 50/50 deal. It's a 100/100 deal, with both of you loving, supporting, and needing the other person.

Men, in particular, need to know that they're needed in a woman's life, and not just any woman—you. Of all the women on the planet, *you* are the only one in his orbit. You figure much higher in his thoughts and in his life than you think.

Consider for a minute how many friends you have. Did you lose track counting? Now think about who your husband hangs out with. How many friends does he have? If he's the average married male, he has one—you. *You* are the one he wants most to understand him. You are the center of his universe, which is why it's important that you, of all people, respect him and need

MAN to MAN

Do yourself a favor. Throw any assumptions you have about women—and specifically your wife—out the window.

Start from scratch. Ask her about what's important to her and how you can support her in those priorities. Admit to her that you're not very comfortable with emotions and feelings but you want to understand what makes her happy and sad.

Be a man and admit, for the sake of your marriage, that you need her to teach you what you should know about her.

him. Show your man that he's needed in your world, and he will always be in your corner. Sure, I know you can open that pickle jar, but allow him to do it for you every once in a while. Every guy likes to flex his muscles in front of his bride.

Ask for his help and allow him to solve problems. It's what he does best. "Hon, I hear a drip coming somewhere from downstairs. Would you mind tracking it down and seeing what's up? I'd appreciate it."

Your guy may not be a plumber or even know which end of the socket wrench he's holding, but he can make that phone call to the local plumber instead of you doing it. And if you want that man of yours to check out that leak even faster, just touch his shoulder and say, "If you could handle that, I'd be able to finish up here, and we could relax together. It's been a long week, hasn't it?"

Everybody loves rewards, and time with you is the ultimate reward to your guy.

Everybody loves rewards, and time with you is the ultimate reward to your guy. It's like throwing a fish to a seal. That seal will perform like nobody's business just to get another fish.

Want to make your man rush home to you—and ignore the part-time young hottie at the office when she tries to get his attention? Then show him your respect and that he's needed. You'll have a husband who is attentive to your every move. He may even surprise you by asking, "What can I do to help?"

Give a little and you'll get a lot back.

Now that's a pretty good deal, don't you think?

To Be Wanted

Ask a man who the most intimidating creature on earth is, and he'll most likely say, "A woman."

That's because women are so capable. They're the multitaskers of the universe. They pull off jobs as CEOs, journalists, bank tellers, and entrepreneurs. During lunch they make doctor appointments and grocery lists while simultaneously munching a sandwich or salad. At home they can diaper the baby, talk on the phone with a girlfriend, clean out the fridge, and place an order on Amazon—all within three minutes.

Us men? Well, we wouldn't even think of doing all those things over lunch because we're singularly focused on one task that we want to do well. During those same three minutes at home, we'd be staring at that diaper, figuring out the best angle to get the tabs to adhere well. Doing the other things wouldn't yet be on our radar. Meanwhile, our spouse has left us in the dust and is down the track doing something else.

Women are so capable. They're the multitaskers of the universe. We men focus on doing one thing at a time.

See why women can be intimidating? You're simultaneously good at many things and organized enough to keep all your ducks in a row. We men focus on doing one thing at a time. Then we move on to the next thing.

In the Leman house, my kids used to groan when it was Dad's turn to cook dinner. I'd yell, "Corn!" and the kids would come to the table and eat corn. Ten minutes later I'd call, "Burgers," and the kids would show up for the next round. We had most of the food groups, but certainly not at the same time.

Now, if Mrs. Uppington made the meal, all food groups not only were represented equally but were served at the same time *and* beautifully arranged on plates, with colorful flowers in the center of the table. Dinner was a work of art.

Even now, decades of marriage later, I'm still amazed at how Sande pulls it off.

With everything you women can do so well—and simultaneously—your husband may sometimes feel like you neither need him nor want him. In fact, he's in the way of you getting things done. You clean his clock every day with your efficiency. He can't begin to compete with all the birthdays, work deadlines, and school papers for your kid that you keep in your head.

So it hurts when you make a snarky remark about him dropping the ball (even if it is your tenth anniversary and he ought to remember). He can't keep as many balls in the air as you can, as much as he tries. But even if he can't keep up with you or the myriad accomplishments in your day, your man wants to know you appreciate the unique roles he plays in your family. He needs to know that you consider him a capable, worthy human being and that he's wanted—utterly important to you personally, to your family, and to your lives together.

Simply stated, he *wants to be wanted*—most of all by you, the one who counts most in his world. Your man wants to please you, like he wanted to please his mama when he was growing up. He just doesn't always know how. That's why I tell women, "Think of your man as a two-year-old who shaves."

Every day, even though he doesn't say it out loud, he's saying, "Show me that you want me." With all the societal changes we discussed earlier, men sometimes feel like they're on the endangered species list. They're often portrayed as not being good enough, made fun of for being stupid and clueless, and gossiped about on girls' nights.

Your man wants to please you. He just doesn't always know how.

Let me ask you this: If your man doesn't feel wanted and needed at home, why would he want to be there? I'll be blunt. No guy wants to be emasculated, especially by the woman he's closest to. Without respect for each other—which comes from understanding each of your needs and wants and working to fulfill them—your marriage is shaky and has no foundation to stand on.

If a man doesn't feel wanted in your universe, he has no reason to work hard to provide for you or to love you in the way you want to be loved. He certainly isn't likely to do *his* part to make changes in his own behavior until you do your part. It's too risky for him to try since he doesn't know if his efforts will be accepted or rejected. And he certainly doesn't want his trials to be reported to your girlfriends and laughed about. His little-boy heart is too tender to take that big of a risk.

Show your guy you want him in your life (yes, that includes sexually) and that no one else can take his place, and you'll have a champion forever. No, he probably can't diaper that baby as fast as you can, though I have seen some heroic efforts by a lot of men. Neither can he heat up soup as fast as you. But let him do those things anyway, without hovering. Or even ask him for his help. I bet you anything he'd be better at researching that new washer and dryer, and it would take at least one item off your to-do list.

So why not simply say to the one who wants to help you the most, "Hon, I've got so much to do today that I'm feeling overwhelmed. Would you mind . . . ?" and let your inbuilt hero rise to the challenge. When the task is complete, say something like, "Wow, I'm so relieved. Because you did that, I was able to get X and X done. I don't know what I'd do without you. You make my world go 'round."

That man of yours will puff out his chest and feel like Superman, even if all he's done is get out the can opener, open the soup, and warm it up in the microwave. Add a kiss for an extra thank-you, and your Superman will be orbiting the moon.

Want the kind of guy who listens patiently to you when you're on a roll about something that's happening at work? Want him

A MAN'S TOP NEEDS

- To be needed.
- To be wanted.
- To be fulfilled.

to be there for you when you're emotionally fragile? Then go for a win-win situation: show him that he's wanted. Loop him in on problems you have without snowing him with information. Ask him for help. Respect him as a *man*—the rock you can count on for support and backup.

Say to him, "Hon, I have a problem at work, and I need your help. You're really good at sorting things out. It's one of the many things I love about you. Would you be willing to hear my thoughts on some solutions and tell me what you think? I don't need you to solve the problem; just listen and let me know if you think there are other angles I could consider."

You probably already know what you're going to do—after all, you're a smart woman. But when you give your husband the opportunity to listen in on your thoughts, you're showing you need him and want his opinion. You're also giving him a peek inside the parts of your world that he otherwise wouldn't see since he's not there.

Note that you aren't asking him to *solve* your problems. You're asking him to listen to solutions you have in mind. Believe me, that's one of the hardest—and most un-male-like—things for a man to do. We men are hardwired to solve problems and tell you what to do.

Be straightforward in your information:

- "Hon, I have a problem."
- Identify who the problem is with. (It's work, not him, so he won't feel defensive.)
- Specify his assignment, which is to listen, not problem-solve.

Then he can be comfortable and confident that he knows the parameters of his job, so he can tackle it and do it well.

And you? Well, you're also gently training that man you love about what you need as a woman—a listening ear, affirmation, a hug, a presence to walk alongside you—all without announcing what you're doing.

See, I told you women are smart.

To Be Fulfilled

I know what you're thinking, and it's a word with three letters. S-E-X.

You're both right and wrong.

Men do think about sex—33 times a day, in fact. The good news is that when your husband thinks about sex, he's also thinking about you. So you should take that as a compliment.

Sexual fulfillment is very important to a man. But stop there. Note that I said "sexual fulfillment," not "sex." There's a difference between simply having sex—an exchange between two physical bodies—and being sexually satisfied because you are experiencing intimacy within a committed, lasting relationship.

In today's society, the act of sex is seemingly free and easy. But outside the bounds of marriage, it's not safe, nor is it emotionally satisfying long-term. The act of sex isn't an end in itself. It's intended to be the culmination of a relationship between two people who love each other and are committed to staying together.

Just being a sexual partner for your spouse isn't enough. For sex to be fulfilling to a husband, he needs a wife who is a *willing* partner, not someone who grudgingly agrees just because she knows she should. That's because sexual fulfillment is connected to the core of a man and his God-given male drive to protect, provide, and care for you.

If you show your desire for and appreciation of your husband as a man, he will never have a reason to look elsewhere. His sexual desires will be fulfilled and completed in your relationship.

So whisper in your husband's ear, "I want you. I need you. You are my man." Don't worry if you have a few extra pounds or any wrinkles. He'll be too busy doing cartwheels to even notice.

With just a little TLC on your part, you'll have a happy, satisfied man. He'll pay more attention to your needs. He'll listen to you. He'll help around the house. He'll tuck those kids in bed. He'll even make midnight runs for those necessary things with wings when you need them.

Want your guy to come running when you call? Then respect him. Show him he's needed. Be an enthusiastic sexual partner.

And you'll have him wrapped around your little pinkie.

What a Woman Needs

What do you think the number-one need of women is?

When I asked that question at a marriage seminar, one man called out, "Visa."

His wife elbowed him, and the rest of the couples laughed.

But what do women long for more than anything? When you see what a woman's top needs are, is it any surprise that sometimes male and female needs collide like two pieces of sandpaper rubbed against each other? Or that friction is the result?

Here are a woman's top three needs.

Affection

Gentlemen, every day your wife is asking you a question, even if she doesn't voice it: *Do you really love me?*

You can answer that question in many ways—words, hugs, caresses, and embraces. However, those physical actions only translate to love and affection for women if they have nothing to do with sex.

Women are very good at sleuthing out the motivation behind any action. Affection to them means hugs, kisses, hand-holding, back rubs, and your presence. It includes affirming words of love and appreciation. Women need affection as *affection*, not just as foreplay. You can't fool them, because their sensitivity radar is always on high. If your wife thinks you're only kissing her to get her into bed, she won't feel truly loved. And if you seem to only be interested in sex, she is going to feel used.

A lot of men are world-class grabbers, but I've yet to meet a woman who says, "I just love it when my husband grabs me."

A woman craves snuggling and sweet somethings whispered in her ear. A man, wired for sexual fulfillment, can't kiss his wife's neck without, well . . . wanting and pushing for more.

See how a woman's need for affection and a man's need for sexual fulfillment can sometimes clash?

Honest, Open Communication

Women thrive on verbal communication. Scientific studies even show that women tend to have more connecting fibers than men between the verbal side of their brains and the emotional side. So what does this mean in the real world of your relationship?

You're dying to hear about your husband's day at work, so you ask, "How did your project go?"

His response: "Gfnnnrrr."

"What exactly does that mean?" you ask.

It means he's not ready to talk about his day at work. He's already used up most of his word count for the day—remember, women use three and a half times more words daily than men—so he's struggling to come up with the remaining ones in his coffer. Also, his feelings haven't yet traveled to his speech center. Yours are zipping along an eight-lane superhighway while his are poking along a little dirt road. They'll get there eventually.

In the meantime, he can only focus on basic human needs. "So, shall we go out for dinner or get takeout?"

Does this mean the two of you can never communicate? No, it means that both of you have to understand what's going on with the other gender.

88

"Why is it he can talk about other things—like the best way to put up drywall or the capabilities of our car engine—but he can't talk to me?" one wife asked me.

Because men are into the details. They're thinking about one project. They can tell you stock prices, interest rates, the size of the trout they caught last summer, or the intricacies of drywall and car engines. Emotions and feelings? That's another matter entirely, and it's tough for men because it's risky.

Unfortunately, stock prices, interest rates, trout, drywall, and car engines put most women to sleep. Emotions are what they care about. That's their turf.

"I want to know how he feels about his job, our future, our family," that same wife told me. "But he never talks about it."

Women need to understand the male lack of communication, but they don't have to settle for it. Communication is the lifeblood of any relationship, and husbands need to step up to that challenge. They can do it; it's just not in their instincts to immediately jump in.

So, guys, take a chance and risk stepping into that unfamiliar territory. If you're really committed to meeting your wife's needs, you have to reach down for your feelings and put them out there on the table. That's what your wife needs.

Your first attempts may not be pretty, but that's okay. You may wind up saying something bumbling like, "I'm not sure how I feel about that. I think maybe I'm kind of excited about my job promotion, but I'm kind of scared too. In a way, I don't want to get my hopes up. You know what I mean?"

You're dying to hear about your husband's day at work, so you ask, "How did your project go?" His response: "Gfnnnrrr."

Granted, that doesn't sound like John Updike's prose (well, actually, it *does* sound like Updike's rambling prose), but it does the job. It opens the door of communication. And the great thing is that she *does* know what you mean. Or if she doesn't, she'll ask. She is the guru of communication, after all.

A WOMAN'S TOP NEEDS

- Affection.
- Honest, open communication.
- Commitment to family.

Hey, you're communicating, so good for you. By making that attempt you're showing your wife you love her enough to share your thoughts and feelings with her, even if you're not good at it.

Wives, for your part, wait for the right time, when your husband's feelings finally chug into the conversational zone. Perhaps you've said things like:

"Why don't you ever talk to me?"

"Can you at least say something?"

"How come you can jabber with your brother on the phone for half an hour in the driveway, but you come inside and you're mute?"

None of those things are helpful. The best thing you can do is be patient. If you are, and you don't pepper him with questions, that man will talk when he's ready. Then you'll be surprised at what you learn as he opens his heart to you.

Commitment to Family

One of the biggest hindrances in marital intimacy is those little critters running around your home. And no, I'm not talking about the dog and the cat.

Any of you with children know that you have to work even harder at marital intimacy once your family expands. Often women do most of the child rearing, even though they're often working full-time or part-time too. Men go full tilt into the role of breadwinner, working 80-hour weeks to make good money so they can buy a posh house in an upscale neighborhood and provide well for their families. Problem is, even if they attain such status, they never see the family who lives there. Their job becomes their life, instead of being a part of their family's life.

Maybe this is what your family is like right now. If so, it's time to take a look at what's most important.

Men, do you really want to be strangers to your family? To be the occasional guest who appears to hand out allowances, tackle discipline, and just assist in major family decisions? Or do you want to be part of the day-to-day workings of your family?

It's tough to be a dad, I know. Women seem to have a natural connection with kids, while many men have to work extra hard to understand their children's needs. But child rearing is a skill that has to be learned, like anything else. If you study the subject a little—which means spending time with your kids, for starters—and ride the learning curve with a little humor, you'll be amazed how fast you'll become a world expert in parenting.

If you were there for the launching, you need to be there for the landing.

Enough said?

Heart to Heart

So, to gain that intimate connection you long for, what's most important?

If You're a Man . . .

Lavish affection—hugs, kisses, and snuggling—on that woman you married. Surprise her with a flower just because you love her. It doesn't have to be a special day like her birthday or your anniversary. Such affection says, "Honey, you're always on my mind and on my heart," even if that work project is vying for top spot in your brain. Doing those kinds of sweet things doesn't make you a wimp. It makes you look even more manly and sexy to that bride of yours. If you're not showing love in the way she receives it, she may not be getting it.

In everything you do, remember she's always asking, "Do you really love me? Do you care?" That's why you shouldn't always expect sex to follow that hugging and kissing. Just do little things she loves because you love her and because affection is her number-one need.

Ask for her opinion. Run things you're thinking of by her first. She may not grasp all the details of an intricate project, but she can give you a valuable perspective.

Take Mike, who had pondered for a week how to add an appropriately sized panel underneath the new oven he'd installed, since it was shorter than the old oven he'd removed. When he asked his wife what she thought, she looked at it for a minute and then said, "You know, it would be really helpful if we had a drawer underneath the oven to store all the bigger pots and pans. Way easier than wrestling them out of the smaller cabinet."

That was a valuable perspective Mike had never thought of. Guys, women in general are closer to life and details like that than we are. So seek out their ideas. They may not know how to install that oven, but they likely know how to use it and everything else in the kitchen.

Talking to your wife is as simple as opening your mouth. Do your best to get past surface levels of communication like, "Wow, it's going to be cold today." Be risky. Try starting a sentence or two with "I feel . . ."

Be risky. Try starting a sentence or two with "I feel . . ."

When she talks, listen first to what she's saying before you try to solve her problems. Maybe she just wants your presence and listening ear. Other times she wants feedback. Listen to what she's asking before you respond.

Listening is hard for us men. Even after all these years of marriage, I still fall into that pattern of not listening sometimes . . .

92

and Sande catches me at it. I show up at the wrong restaurant when I'm supposed to meet her for dinner because I tuned her out earlier.

We men tend to tune out our wives if we think we're not getting new information—emphasis on the word *think*. But we miss reading *how* our wives say things in the flurry of all they're telling us.

So, men, hear the facts, but also listen for and watch for the feelings. That means you stop what you're doing and focus on her when she's talking. Then ask questions to clarify what she said. When you do, you'll be amazed at how much less she'll have to talk. If you're actually listening, she can get her point across faster. If you look her in the eyes, she'll know you heard her and will follow through on something you need to get done.

Make a point to be home, and engage when you're home. Be helpful with the kids and household tasks, and show commitment to your family as a whole. When you spend time with your kids, it's like hugging your wife. She's called Mama Bear for a reason—she always has her cubs in mind. But without the rock-solid presence of Papa Bear by her side, she's flailing out there on her own, trying to fulfill the cubs' needs and keep them in check.

Above all, memorize these words: "How can I help, honey?" Acts of love truly are the golden key to marital bliss.

If You're a Woman . . .

Remember that men, by nature, are solitary critters. Treat your husband like your best friend and he'll become your biggest fan. Just because you're married doesn't mean you should stop dating. Go along with him on the activities he enjoys. If you learn to like the things he does, like certain sports, that's even better. But it's not necessary. Just be there. Be his companion.

When Sande and I were dating, she told me she loved to fish. Later, I realized *I* was the fish. When I'd take her on a fishing trip, she'd lie down on the boat. For her, it was a time to relax and for us to talk about what mattered. For me, it was time to catch some fish. As a wise professor of mine once said, "As a couple you can do different things . . . together."

Don't expect your husband to be your girlfriend, who can chat for hours about a subject. Give him the highlights and wait for his brain to catch up before you move on to a new topic.

Let him be your hero. Openly respect him as a male and admire his masculine qualities. (What guy doesn't love to flex his muscles in front of his woman?)

Show him through your actions that he's important in your family's life. Tell him he fills a role that nobody else does. Say "thank you" for the things he does.

Let him be your hero.

Save time just for him and pay attention to his emotional, physical, and sexual needs. Fulfill those and put him first, and he'll even run through a brick wall for you if that's what it takes.

I once saw a cartoon with two birds on a branch. One of them had that amorous Bullwinkle look in his eye. The other bird said, "I know we're lovebirds, but I still have a headache."

Remember that men need to be needed—and part of that is to be needed sexually. Don't just "put up with" or go through the motions of sex. Having sex with your husband isn't a marital duty; it's a privilege and the culmination of your growing love. Instead, be an active participant in the process. Enjoy it and creatively please him.

One woman told me how, at the urging of her girlfriends, she decided to plan something especially fun for her husband, who was returning home from a long business trip. So, to meet him as soon as he disembarked from his plane (this was prior to the security changes prompted by 9/11) at the airport, she wore a trench coat and basically nothing else. It was a great plan—until the metal detector went off.

The security guard couldn't understand why she refused to take off her coat, but they finally determined it was the belt that set off the alarm and let her through. She won't be trying that again anytime soon.

To this day, she and her husband laugh about that event. And he greatly appreciated her efforts to please him.

You don't have to go quite that far, but what *can* you do?

Break out of your comfort zone a little. Try some things you've never done before.

My wife is a very private person who observes what I call the Half-Mile Rule. We can't have sex if there's anyone within a half mile. If a neighbor's garage door opens down the street, she shuts down. She's worried someone will hear us.

> *Break out of your comfort zone a little. Try some things you've never done before.*

Me? A dump truck could drive into the bedroom and I wouldn't care because I'd be circling the moon.

So when Sande goes out of her way to surprise me, I fall in love with her all over again because I know the effort it took for her to do so.

A lot of things you'd like your husband to do for you won't come naturally either, like talking and sharing his heart. But to please each other, you have to take some risks. So try a little creativity. He'll love your efforts. Trust me.

Do those things, ladies and gentlemen, and people who see your interaction will be asking you for marriage advice.

SECRET #6

Sex Is Important . . . but Not for the Reasons You Might Think

How this culminating act of intimacy reflects personal views and needs and impacts marital health.

How's your sex life?

Yes, that's a blunt question, but I'm asking it because sexual fulfillment has everything to do with the health of your marriage. In all my years of professional counseling, I've never heard a couple say, "Doc, we haven't had sex for a while, but we're just fine with that. We're still happily married."

Sexual expression is a vital part of the love that brings a man and a woman together as husband and wife in the first place and keeps them connected. Without it, an essential ingredient for a satisfied relationship is missing.

Problem is, many of us were taught or learned by osmosis in childhood that sex is bad, dirty, and a subject that shouldn't be openly discussed. Yes, most people did it—at least if you believe everything on the internet—but only a few bold people talked about it.

How did you learn about sex? Through a warm, open, loving discussion with your mom and dad? That hardly ever happens. Instead, one of your parents might have said uncomfortably, "Uh, we need to have a talk about . . . you know . . . ," because they read that they should do that in an article or online somewhere. They didn't know what to say because their parents didn't talk to them about sex either. Or you learned the basics from your middle school class, where boys and girls eyed each other and giggled.

Today, though, that uncomfortable conversation and middle school class come far after everything you already know through googling, seeing things written on public restroom walls, and getting the scoop from "knowledgeable" peers. I don't need to tell you all the nicknames for male and female parts; you've already heard them. But what do they say about our feelings toward sex? As much as we're bombarded by sexual images today, we're uncomfortable with "real" words like *penis* and *vagina*. And why is it that the nicknames for male private parts tend to be comical but the ones for females are derogatory or barely talked about?

Superior-Inferior Attitude Check

Flash back to high school for a minute, and pretend you're standing in the guys' locker room. It's a Monday after school, and the team's changing clothes. Ignore the sweaty-sock odor and just focus on the conversation.

"Hey, Justin!" one player yells. "Did you get any this weekend?"

Justin puffs up a little. "Yeah. I got more than a little." He smiles. "I scored."

And when we're talking score, we're not talking basketball.

Think about the words those boys are using for sex: *got* and *scored*. Do those sound like loving, caring words that would make a girl feel special? Or more like a competitive game that the boys are out to win?

Many people today, and especially the younger generations, tend to think of sex as a competition—a taking-from rather than a giving-to experience. For someone to win, someone else has to lose. The question isn't "How much can I give to the other person or do for her?" Rather, it's "How much can I get for myself?"

That kind of competition breeds the type of society where others are viewed as sex objects or things to be used. But people should never be used like temporary dust cloths and then thrown away.

For someone to win, someone else has to lose.

Anytime sex is used as a weapon to conquer or overcome feelings of inferiority, to repay a favor, to perform a duty, to gain attention or power, or to win a battle in marriage, it won't be fulfilling for either partner. In marriage, there should be no place for superior or inferior roles. There should only be mutual love and respect. Part of that love and respect is understanding each other's needs, which we went over in the last chapter, and fulfilling them.

When Male and Female Needs Intersect

If you ask men, "What's the most special physical act a man can engage in with a woman?" I know hands down what they'd say. So do you.

But if you ask women that same question, you'll get a completely different answer. For women, the most special act is being held—gently and tenderly. Does that mean she can't enjoy sex? Absolutely not. She's capable of receiving immense pleasure from sexual love *as long as she has a partner who makes her feel loved and cherished.* Did you catch that, men?

The problems begin when husband and wife don't understand some basic physical differences.

Men in general are much more easily aroused by sight than women are. That's why magazines and online sites featuring nude women flourish. Men aren't reading them for the interesting articles or viewing them to glimpse any beautiful images of romantic love. They also aren't as likely to read Danielle Steel novels, where the male hero burns with passion for the heroine, so he goes anywhere, does anything, and even suffers any injustice in order to win the woman's hand. No, instead a man's sexual interest begins with the mere sight of an attractive female, a suggestive picture, or a seductive look.

Contrast that to women, who feel their hearts beat faster when their guy gives them a hug and holds them. Not that they don't look at the cover package of men—especially today's younger generation, who can ogle good-looking hunks across the world on their iPhones—but it's usually not as high on females' radar. There's a reason females tell me they tend to look first at arm muscles, abs, eyes, and mouths. They rarely ever mention how attractive a winkie is. (Yet men the planet over still compare the size of theirs, thinking that matters to women.)

My wife, for instance, has always claimed that I'm much sexier with my clothes on than off. Some night I'm going to sneak under the covers in my best suit and bellow my mating call. But I doubt that would "get her in the mood" in the same way that doing sweet things for her throughout the day would.

Do you know how tough it is for a man to just hold a woman? When I hold my wife, about 4.3 seconds later my little Black and Decker begins to crank up. My caveman impulses want to take over. Then there's Sande, who might take 43 minutes of me holding her to warm up.

So how can couples handle such a dichotomy?

Flash back to that Danielle Steel novel for a moment. Millions of those books sell because readers are sighing dreamily and wishing the men in their lives were more like those fantasy characters. What woman wouldn't want her male hero to express his love so eloquently that she can fall into bed with him with ease?

What's my point, men? Simply that a woman needs to hear a man tell her how much he loves her. She needs him to tell her how thankful he is that she's a part of his life. She needs to know how beautiful she looks that night, or to be told, "I love you even more today than I did the day we got married. You'll always be my girl."

If you love your wife, tell her. Is being in bed with her the greatest feeling you've ever experienced—one that draws you back to her side? Then tell her that. You don't have to be eloquent. You don't have to talk sexy. Yes, she may be better at expressing herself, but that doesn't mean you can't learn to do better.

And don't forget that sex doesn't begin in the bedroom. It begins in the kitchen and anywhere else you intersect, and it continues throughout the day.

It begins when you remember to take the garbage out and pick up your dirty socks and put them in the laundry where they belong. It continues when you rub your wife's back and give her a sweet kiss as you make her coffee in the morning before you both go out the door. It continues when you text her, "I'm thinking about you" over lunch. It ramps up when you add, "Don't worry about picking up that dessert for the party tonight. I know what you like. I'll pick it up and meet you at home."

Let me tell you something. Do those sweet things throughout the day, and you'll both be in the mood and will hurry home from that party.

Marriage is all about needs. You have to meet the immediate needs of your wife *first* or you won't have the opportunity to service her more intimate needs. That means you have to build a track record of showing your wife how much you care about her. To her, all those little things are important.

If your wife is home with small children all day, the vacuum cleaner is plugged, and the baby eats a dead ladybug off the rug, what do you think the immediate need on her mind will be? To unplug that vacuum cleaner, of course! See, you're a rocket scientist.

Then the two-year-old got into the paint you intended for the garage walls, and your wife has spent three hours trying to get that paint off her favorite white bedspread. So what should you be doing this weekend? Painting those garage walls and getting rid of the leftover paint. When you do those two things for your wife, she knows you care and that you're interested in the details of her everyday life.

A woman needs to know she's your number-one choice, not the runner-up when you have time to take care of something.

What about Celibate Marriages?

Jason, a man in his midthirties, came to see me. He wanted to start a family but wasn't sure how to talk about that with his wife, a corporate CEO who was frequently on business trips. With both of them focusing on the fast track to success, they hadn't made love for several years. Jason told me he was feeling lonely.

"I thought we could do things in stages—get our careers settled, then focus on a family," he said.

"How's that working for you?" I asked.

He sighed. "Well, I thought it was working fine. But . . . somewhere along the way we lost our interest in each other."

Sex is an intimate act that culminates from the closeness a couple has developed.

When sex is removed from the marital equation, something's off in the relationship. That couple's priority wasn't figuring out how to have a baby. They had to work on their relationship first, honestly communicating needs and feelings to each other *before* sex and making a baby could even come into the picture. Sex is the glue that keeps a marriage together and protects it against other temptations, but it's not an end in

MAN to MAN

Sex isn't a business, where you can judge results and then do the same thing time after time to get a proven track record. It can't be approached that way. For your wife to feel loved, you have to create the right conditions first, which means being gentle, loving, and caring, and putting her priorities first. That goes against what you've grown up thinking—that to be a man, you have to be aggressive and rough-and-tumble.

If you become too aggressive, rough, or hurried, most likely your wife's systems will automatically shut down. That's because she first needs to feel affection—nonsexual touching—and a lot of it, to prepare her. It's also because her clitoris, which has dozens of nerve endings, is highly sensitive and must be touched in a soft, gentle manner. If you do so, it fills with blood and becomes erect, much like your penis. But touch it too hard and it hurts.

Also, throw the idea of simultaneous orgasms out the window. Yes, it does happen for some couples, but it isn't common. Usually for a woman to have one at all, hers must come first as a result of manual stimulation of her clitoris, before the male inserts his penis into her vagina.

The goal for sexual fulfillment should be to enjoy each other to the maximum without putting expectations on this wonderful union. Expecting your wife to orgasm the same time as you, or even at all, is unrealistic because of the cycles of a woman's body. So don't take the spontaneity and beauty out of sex by adding pressure to perform.

If the two of you are too busy trying to stay within "the rules" you create, you can't enjoy the sport. What's important is that you are both satisfied with the closeness of your physical union at that time.

itself. Sex is an intimate act that culminates from the closeness a couple has developed.

Celibacy between married couples is simply not normal or healthy. Yes, in times of high stress a couple may mutually agree on no sex for a time. But after that agreed-upon time, without engaging in sex the couple will drift apart, like Jason and his wife had.

FOR
WOMEN ONLY

Some of you have been taught while growing up that, to be attractive to a male, you have to be sweet, soft, and follow a man's lead. But do you know what that husband of yours secretly wants you to be? Sexually assertive! Remember—your guy needs to be needed. There's not a man out there who doesn't want to feel prized, loved, and sexually desirable.

That means sometimes your guy wants *you* to start the action. Sex isn't a spectator sport, where one party sits back and waits for the action to begin on the field. For sex to be mutually fulfilling, it has to be both comfortable and exciting to both of you.

So get comfortable with your own body. Knowing what feels pleasurable to you will help you steer your husband in the way he should go. What feels good on Friday won't feel good on Monday, since your hormones and cycles are constantly changing. Also, women thrive on variety whereas men thrive on routine. So do what you're best at—get creative.

When your husband arrives home, *you* take action sometimes. Plant a big kiss on him that's more than a peck. Since you're the verbal master, let him know right then and there that you're interested in his body. I seriously doubt there's a man alive today who hasn't had a single fantasy about his wife meeting him at the door with such a scene . . . or wearing nothing.

My wife, in fact, got even more creative. One summer Friday I arrived home, exhausted from the week. I should have suspected from the beginning that something was up because I didn't see the children in front of the house. They were usually sitting out on the front rocks, trying to decide whose turn it was to help me steer the car up the driveway.

When I walked into the house, I knew something was amiss. The dining room table was set with the best china (dishes that don't bounce if you drop them), and the stereo was playing soft music.

Attached to the back door was a piece of red yarn, which ran down to a note taped to the floor: "Follow this red string and you'll find a beautiful thing."

So I threw down my clothes—er, briefcase—and followed that red yarn like a puppy, all the way into the bathroom. There I found another note that read, "Not here, dummy. Try the bed."

Sure enough, there was a beautiful thing on the bed—my wife. She'd gone out of her way to let me know how special I was in her life. You'd have to know Sande to appreciate the fact that this sort of thing is not her style, but she did it anyway—including arranging for the kids to spend the evening at Grandma's.

We never did have dinner on those china plates, but I felt really special that evening. And it's a night I'll never forget because my wife showed me how much she loved me.

Couples give me a lot of excuses for why they *don't* have sex, including time, busyness, and neither feels like it. Instead, they should look for opportunities to have sex as a part of their intimate connection. Sometimes they have to get creative.

One couple I know had to find new ways to engage in sexual intimacy when the husband, a construction worker, was paralyzed after falling from a three-story roof. Another limited-income couple who had no family in their area was surprised by a set of twins back-to-back with their first child. But in between the crying and feeding of babies, they found exciting new ways to explore each other's bodies. Because the husband, who worked three part-time jobs to bring home the bacon, was sexually fulfilled, he eagerly rushed home to help his wife every day. He told her how much he loved and appreciated her. As a result, that young mom was happy and content even with her exhausting schedule of caring for three young children and finding ways to stretch a dollar.

Now those are win-win situations.

Frequency and Creativity

"How often should we have sex?" couples often ask. "Once a week? Five times a week? Once a month?"

The frequency is up to the two of you, as long as it's mutually agreeable, respects both of your needs, and focuses on the desire to please each other. Some partners crave once-a-day sex. Others like it once a month. What's important is that you talk about your needs and decide together how to handle them.

If you focus on pleasing each other, you can weather all the different stages of marriage—including infertility, miscarriage, pregnancy, jobs gained and lost, little ankle biters entering the picture, and cranky in-laws—because you've retained your intimate connection with each other.

An Unbreakable Bond

Sexual fulfillment is a powerful, extremely personal experience that triggers strong emotions and bonds you to your partner. That's why it's so important to a married couple—and even more so if this is your second or third time around the block with a marriage partner, if you've had any previous sexual experiences, or if you two were living together before you said "I do."

No matter what your previous sexual experiences were, today is a new day. You can start fresh. Sex is more than fun, something you do because you have to, or a way to relieve boredom on a Friday night. Think of sex with your spouse as a marital superglue that bonds you deeply, making it tough for any other forces to tear you apart.

Instead of watching a romantic movie, make your own. Instead of reading a Danielle Steel book and wishing your relationship was like that, create your own passionate plot. Let the pieces of it unfold throughout the day so that when you see each other at night, both of your engines are already revving. Then, keeping each other's needs in mind, get creative.

Instead of watching a romantic movie, make your own.

Sex doesn't have to begin in the bedroom. It's an all-day affair of meeting each other's needs so you both enjoy the culmination . . . whether it's in the living room, kitchen, or garage. It can even be outside in a hastily assembled tent, if you feel adventuresome.[1]

Then again, you might have to keep an eye out for spiders.

SECRET #7

To Love Your Spouse, You Have to Know Who You Married

Understand birth order and you can use it to your shared benefit.

I made a mistake—a whopping marital mistake. Yesterday I told Sande, my lovely bride, that a TV crew was coming to our home today to tape an interview with me.

I ought to have known better. I've been married to the same incredible woman for over four decades, so you'd think I would have learned something by now. As soon as I tell her someone is coming to our house, she immediately thinks, *What am I going to serve them? Hmm . . . maybe pulled pork sandwiches and a fruit salad? Yeah, that might work. And for dessert . . .* Then she catches sight of the windows, which have a miniscule smudge of dirt. *Oh no, they're a mess. Why does he do things like this?*

But why do I say it's a "marital mistake"? Because from the instant I announced that visit to my wife, she's kept me break-neck busy. I've been told, "Leemie, sweep the front deck and back porch. Clean the windows and get the spiderwebs off. And don't forget—pick up the dog flops from the yard." Even our son-in-law Josh, who's visiting, got roped in to clean the first-floor bathroom.

So why did I tell her at all? I've learned the hard way over the years that my wife doesn't like surprises. Telling her the morning of that someone is coming would result in, if not death, then certainly critical wounds to my body.

To Sande, a kitchen is only truly clean when all surface areas are wiped off and the toaster is put away. My thinking is, *Why put away a toaster when you're going to use it within the next 24 hours?* After all, I'm a guy, and I eat the same thing every day. I'm comfortable with that routine.

Fact is, Sande and I both have BO—birth order—and understanding it has had everything to do with developing an intimate connection that has lasted through five kids, three marriages of those kids, and four grandkids.

As I said earlier, men and women clearly are different. You women are multitasking queens with complicated brain patterns that make us men dizzy. We are more simple, one-thing-at-a-time thinkers and doers. But achieving marital harmony is far more than merely understanding the differences between men and women. With just a little knowledge about your own birth order and your spouse's, you can have the kind of marriage that makes others say, "Wow, I want one of those!"

Who Are You?

I have a few simple questions for you. With your answers, I can guess quite a bit about you, including how you respond to situations and the way you interact with your spouse. Nine times out of ten I'm right. Want to try it out to see how I do with you? Then take the quick quiz below.

Which group do you most closely identify with?

Group #1: You're . . .

- a natural leader
- logical and technical
- conscientious and a list maker
- a perfectionist

Group #2: You're . . .

- self-motivated and you like to do things yourself
- a high achiever, expecting a lot out of yourself
- a regular user of words like *always* and *never*
- allergic to the idea of failure

Group #3: You're . . .

- the mediator when family or friends fight
- a master at avoiding conflict
- loyal to your friends
- independent and good at keeping secrets

Group #4: You're . . .

- friendly and you connect easily with others
- the one who got away with everything in your family because you were "cute"
- affectionate in your words and body language
- someone who thrives in the spotlight

Now let me be your armchair psychologist.

If you picked Group #1, you're most likely the first child (or the first child of your gender) born in your family.

If you picked Group #2, chances are high you're an only child. You've got all the qualities of a firstborn child, but they're heightened in intensity.

If you picked Group #3, you're a middle child.

If you picked Group #4, you're a lastborn or baby of your family.

How can I make such guesses? Because I've seen these character traits of different birth orders play out time and time again over many years. Birth order, though, isn't an exact science since not all character traits fit every person in that birth order. Also, there are exceptions—variables that actually change your birth order. These include:

- physical and/or emotional differences that cause one child to usurp another's role
- the gender of the children (a firstborn boy and firstborn girl in a family will likely both have firstborn tendencies, whereas two boys result in a firstborn and a middle or baby)
- years between the children (five or more years between children starts a new "family," since they don't have to compete)
- a miscarriage or death of a child, which affects the sibling closest in age, if any
- blended families, which toss birth order into a blender
- the critical eye of parents (the most profound birth-order-changing variable of all)

Why You Are the Way You Are

Why is it so important to know and understand your birth order? Because the order in which you were born—and the role you played in your family—has everything to do with how you perceive reality. That, in turn, greatly affects how you view and respond to your spouse.

As you seek to understand your spouse—anticipating their needs and fulfilling their desires—birth order provides a secret window into your partner's world and heart. It prompts those aha moments: "Ah, now I know why he reacts that way when I say X and X!" When you have those secrets stashed in your back pocket, you can then get on the front end of any disagreement before it becomes an argument. And because you know why your spouse is the way he is, you can choose to proactively *respond* instead of blindly reacting.

Firstborns rule.

Middleborns mediate.

Lastborns charm.

Nothing in life is cookie-cutter, though, and birth order isn't either. But understanding the basics will give you clues about why each of you thinks, feels, and acts the way you do. No one acts out of a void. You learned to be the person you are based on the way your parents and siblings interacted with you. The little girl or boy you once were, you still are, as I'll reveal to you next.

Firstborns Rule

If you are a firstborn, you were the family guinea pig. Your parents tried out all their new parenting techniques on you. You also were the doer of all the "firsts": the first child to eat dead ladybugs off the floor, first one to walk, first one to go to kindergarten, first one to plunge into puberty, first one to drive, first one to go on a date. With the spotlight of parental expectations beamed on you, is it any wonder you're a perfectionist?

Firstborns are well-organized list makers. They're born leaders with a lot of practice, since they were held responsible for their siblings. They love books and tend to take life very seriously. They constantly feel the pressure to be better and do better. They are often critical of themselves and of others. And they don't like surprises—they need details and specific time frames.

If you're an onlyborn, you're a supercharged firstborn. Just take all the firstborn qualities times 10, and that's you. Plus you can't understand why siblings fight.

If you're a firstborn:

- Work hard on lightening up! Realize that not everyone has the high need for control that you do, and that your expectations could be set too high. If you're always picking specks of lint off your mate's clothing, it's time to stop. I know it's the little things that drive you up the wall, but would the world really end if a speck of lint resided there? Or if you actually bought a brownie mix instead of trying to make brownies from scratch?

- Go easy on criticism and correction—of both yourself and others. Ask your husband or wife for input on decisions: "How do you feel about that?" "What do you think about that?"

- Remember that marriage is not a one-person show; it's a partnership. Because you tend to prioritize things and deadlines over people, it is easy to settle into arm's-length relationships. But marriage is not an arm's-length gig, nor is it a competitive sport. If you think you're winning in your marriage, you're actually losing.

- Focus on serving your mate, attending to their needs. You have marvelous leadership skills, and you can lead by example.

- Do your best to find and see the humor in situations that you might at first think are disastrous. Laughter truly is the best medicine for any relationship.

If you're married to a firstborn:

- Take pressure off your spouse whenever you can. Don't assume just because he always does something that he should do it.

- Provide specific details, times, and facts for upcoming events, purchases, or other situations.

- Find ways to encourage laughter, fun, and time off.

112

- Keep your living space organized, streamlined, and decluttered.
- Provide perspective on failures. Firstborns tend to emphasize failures and not give themselves enough credit for successes. Celebrate both little and big successes together.

Middleborns Mediate

If you are a middleborn, you took one look at the star firstborn above you and decided, *There's no way I can compete with that. I'm doing my own thing.* Most likely you went in the opposite direction of your firstborn sibling. You were stuck in the middle, so you learned early in life how to make peace between your warring siblings. Since you were least likely to be noticed as missing from the dinner table, is it any surprise you focused on friendships and were very loyal to your friends?

Middleborns are great diplomats. They avoid conflict and like the pathways of life to be smooth. They are independent, walk to the beat of a different drummer, and tend to keep secrets from family members. They don't often share feelings and are surprised when people pay attention to them.

If you're a middleborn:

- Realize that you have something unique to contribute to your family. Your presence matters.
- Remember that what you think and feel counts as much as your partner's opinion.
- When you want to withdraw from conflict, take a deep breath. Stand up for yourself.
- Step outside your comfort zone to share your opinion. Chances are it will be a brand-new perspective others didn't think of.

If you're married to a middleborn:

- Be patient in drawing out your secretive, quieter spouse. Ask often, "What do you think?" and say, "I'd love your opinion on this." Because as a middle child he was often lost in the shuffle growing up, he needs to know his thoughts and feelings matter to you and that his role in the family is important.

- Realize that a middleborn wants the road of life to be smooth, so it's easy to take advantage of her. She'll naturally take the path of least resistance.

- Take time to get to know him—what motivates him, makes him smile.

- Since friends are greatly important, make sure she has time with friends no matter how busy life gets. Most of all, work to become her loyal *friend* as well as her partner.

Lastborns Charm

If you are a lastborn, you grew up as the cute baby who was the apple of every family member's eye. You learned quickly how to manipulate your older siblings into doing your share of the workload, but they also used you to get what they wanted from your parents. After all, who could say no to you? You are the entertainer, the charmer everyone loves, the party waiting to happen. Your life mantra is, "Don't worry. Be happy."

Lastborns are people persons who could sell anything. They're affectionate and engaging. They could charm the socks off an elephant. They love to be the center of attention, and "Surprise" is their middle name. They tend to act impulsively and sometimes think through consequences later.

If you're a lastborn:

- Realize that although life is a thrill ride to you, not everyone sees it that way. Some, like middleborns, like the pathways of life smooth as glass, without the roller-coaster bumps and turns.

- You may love spontaneity, but your partner, especially if he is a firstborn, needs to know details of activities in advance.

(And by "in advance," I don't mean saying, "Oh, honey, we have to be at X in five minutes.")

- Try experiencing some slower days with just your spouse and one activity (instead of a dozen).
- Planning ahead won't kill you . . . and your spouse will thank you.

If you're married to a lastborn:

- Remember that dropping the ball or telling you last-minute about activities doesn't mean your spouse doesn't take you seriously or care about you. It's simply part of the psyche of a baby of the family. Because she's that way, she assumes everybody else is . . . until you tell her differently (nicely, of course).
- Prompt him when needed to fulfill tasks he's agreed to do. He's used to others doing his work for him. If you're newly married, he's majorly on a learning curve. However, giving him grace doesn't mean you do a job for him.
- Realize that babies of the family need parameters. When you need her to be serious, tell her that. When she needs to be somewhere on time, tell her why, and say it's important to you.
- When a bill needs to be paid, have someone who isn't a baby of the family pay it. Then it's more likely to get done. (If both of you are lastborns, you might need to hire a tax accountant.)

Birth Order Matches

Now that you understand the basics of birth order, how does it play out in your relationship? And what can you practically do to handle the inevitable clashes that otherwise would result?

Firstborn + Firstborn

It's inevitable that two firstborns—who are perfectionistic and have a high need for control—will bump heads from time to time. To reduce tension and create harmony, first define your roles carefully. For example: Who will take out the garbage? Who will mow the lawn? Who is responsible for car repair? Who will balance the checking account? Specific lists will avoid arguments over control. Remind yourself that marriage is a partnership—not an "I'm doing it my way" song. Prune the words "You should . . ." out of your vocabulary. Instead of "improving" on things your mate says and does, say, "Thank you." When a criticism pops into your mind, think through the consequences before you speak. If you do these things, together you can take on the world and accomplish phenomenal things.

Firstborn + Middleborn

A firstborn is strong in opinion and outspoken. A middleborn is secretive with opinions and emotions, wanting to keep the highways of life smooth. It's important that the two of you set up regular times where you discuss events and feelings. A typical middleborn response is, "Everything is fine." But "fine" won't make a marriage hum. Work on establishing an environment where both of you affirm each other and share feelings on events. If you're the firstborn, this starts with you stepping forward and saying, "What do you think?" and "Tell me how you really feel. I want to hear more." If you're the middleborn, as one who is perceptive and a good mediator, realize that you have wonderful problem-solving skills that are greatly needed and appreciated. You have so much to offer!

Firstborn + Lastborn

You've got the best of all worlds. Sande and I ought to know, because this is us. Firstborns provide structure, goals, and organization that can be lacking with lastborns, and lastborns heighten the much-needed fun quotient for overly serious firstborns. If you're the firstborn, encourage your lastborn mate to do their share of the work. When you spot flaws, let them go or gently suggest how to correct them. If you're the lastborn, remember that your firstborn mate needs attention and strokes, even if they don't act like it. And to keep the marital waters smooth, before you do anything, make sure you run it by your detailed spouse first.

Middleborn + Middleborn

Neither of you is big on confrontation, and you've been reared to discount your opinions. So you both need to work hard at showing each other respect. Do things that make your spouse feel special and build up their self-worth. Find a fun way to swap emotional happenings. One middleborn couple I know writes notes on slips of paper about important happenings when they're both traveling for work. They use them as discussion starters for their next meals together. Since friendships are important to both of you, provide plenty of space for outside relationships. However, don't forget the most important relationship—the two of you.

Middleborn + Lastborn

Middleborns like relationships to be smooth; lastborns like fun. But both birth orders specialize in friendships. To keep your marriage thriving, if you're the middleborn, develop and blend your social interests with what your lastborn spouse thinks is fun. If you're the lastborn, back off from always being in the spotlight and allow your middleborn spouse to shine. Above all, develop shared interests that you both enjoy and work on making the other person feel pampered and special.

Lastborn + Lastborn

Since neither of you is detail oriented and you're used to others doing things for you, do something completely foreign to you: make a list. Decide who will do what, including cooking, cleaning the house, shopping, and organizing the social calendar. If responsibilities are down on paper, there can't be any misunderstanding or passing the buck of blame. Listen to what your spouse says not only with their eyes but with their body language. Hold each other accountable (it'll be a new experience for both of you), and maximize your sense of humor. Laugh often. It takes the sting out of the bill-paying process, which neither of you will like but one or both of you has to do.

Two Becoming One

Good marriages are made, not instant, when you say "I do." A thriving marriage requires two people working together in a caring, mutually supportive environment. Think of it this way: If you were both the same, there wouldn't be a need for one of you. Those differences that can frustrate you are also what make you a couple, so why not enjoy them?

To gain that intimate connection you long for—a marriage that's better than you can ever dream—you have to get behind your spouse's eyes and see how they view life. You need to care about what they care about, even if their reality is completely different from yours. To become one as a couple, you have to engage their heart.

If you were both the same, there wouldn't be a need for one of you.

When you understand birth order, the strengths and weaknesses of each other, and how your mate sees life as a result, you set the stage for your marriage to soar into a relationship better than you could ever dream.

Backtrack to my wife and the TV crew story from the beginning of this chapter. After all that work, the reporter and camera guy were only at our home for one and a half hours. But my wife, always the perfect hostess, offered them coffee, and life went on happily. The reporter, eight months pregnant, did make several runs to the freshly cleaned bathroom, so at least that got the notice it deserved.

In hindsight, what would this free-wheeling baby of the family have done differently in relating to his cautious firstborn wife? I would have told her a week prior to the TV crew's visit—enough time for her to get the menu happily laid out and feel comfortable with it and for me to do all those cleaning tasks she pointed out without having to be on a 24-hour kamikaze schedule. Want your marriage to thrive? Then take time to understand your partner's birth order.[1] See life as they see it. If something is important to them, it has to be important to you, even if it means a boatload of housecleaning.

And don't forget those dog flops in the yard either.

SECRET #8

Clashes Feel Less Personal When You Understand Your Partner's Personality

How personality types influence the way each of you views life and your relationship.

Did you know that your basic personality was already formed by first grade? And that the little kid you were then is likely much the same as the adult you are now? That's what a research study that tracked personalities of people for 40 years said. The study looked at how much the individuals talked, how adaptable they were, whether they were controlled or impulsive, and whether they were confident or "self-minimizing."[1]

Personality is "a part of us, a part of our biology," study author Christopher Nave concluded.[2] It's a very interesting part indeed. The more you understand about your partner's personality, the less personal any clashes in your marriage will seem. That in itself will make your differences much easier to navigate.

The Four Basic Personalities at Their Best and Worst

Personality has been a fascinating subject of study for over 2,000 years. People always are curious about why they do what they do and what makes other people tick—especially those who are very different from them and who they have to relate to on a daily basis. Two thousand years ago, in fact, Hippocrates—one smart cookie—identified four basic categories of personalities, which he called *temperaments*. Even today, those four temperaments are still reliable descriptions of basic personality types:

- sanguine
- choleric
- melancholic
- phlegmatic

An easy way to remember the overall differences in the types is this story:

> Four people . . . see a star fall to earth. The Sanguine talks about it animatedly to all present; the Choleric wants to form an expedition to find it and analyze it; the Melancholic ponders what it means and how he feels about it; and the Phlegmatic waits for the others to decide what to do as whatever decision they make is fine by him.[3]

Which response sounds most like you? Which one sounds most like your partner? Well then, you already have a basic idea of each of your personality types, but below are the highlights.

Sanguine: "Let's do it the fun way."

If you're a *sanguine*, you'll tend to be more social and fun-loving. You're comfortable in a crowd, you smile a lot, and you could engage anyone in a conversation. You also have a good sense of humor, possess the ability to tell wonderful stories, and are usually playful and happy. "Spontaneity" is your middle name. You jump into anything with both feet first and ask questions later.

Your needs are social-based. More than anything you want to be noticed and appreciated. You live for approval. If someone adores you, even better.

Your weaknesses? You are often disorganized, are not good with details, and sometimes exaggerate a bit when you tell stories. You're likely late to meetings or miss them altogether. You're fun to have around, but your "Why worry? Just be happy!" attitude sometimes drives those who are more serious and work oriented a wee bit crazy, especially if they end up having to do your work for you. But if you're rejected, it hits home hard. When you encounter stress, you tend to exit stage left quickly, go on a spending spree, or find someone who does approve of you. If you can't leave, you'll create some sort of excuse—not always buyable—or try to pass the buck of blame. You hate being bored, have a short attention span, and would never dream of putting yourself on a budget (if something looks good, you buy it) or figuring out how long it takes to get anywhere (hey, you just get there when you get there).

> *Your needs are social-based. More than anything you want to be noticed and appreciated. You live for approval. If someone adores you, even better.*

If your spouse is a sanguine, what are the worst ways to respond to them?

- Criticize their actions or unfulfilled promises. (They live for approval.)
- Tell them, "Not everybody thinks you're cute." (They'll be in the dumps for the entire day.)
- Don't laugh at their silly antics or jokes.

123

What are the best ways to respond?

- Show an active interest in them.
- Appreciate the way they can motivate, entertain, and inspire people—just don't expect them to be detail oriented or always follow through on what they say they'll do.
- If they drop the ball on being where they should be at the time they should be, gently point that out. But also point out their good qualities and how much they mean to you.
- Find creative ways to remind them where they should be and when.
- Laugh at their silly antics or jokes. (They love being in the limelight.)

Jan's married to a sanguine who often forgets where he should be when, especially if he's in the middle of telling coworkers an entertaining story after work. So she tried a new strategy. He loves coffee, but they're on a budget, and $5 a day for their local coffee drive-through isn't on it. So she bought some cheap to-go cups with lids and a silver Sharpie. Every day she writes a note on the lid, such as, "See you at 6 at Outback Steakhouse." Then she draws a heart. Every time he lifts that coffee cup to drink, he's reminded not only of where he wants to be (the idea gets implanted in his brain and lodges there) but also that Jan loves him.

Kudos to that smart woman.

Choleric: "Let's do it my way."

If you're a *choleric*, you're confident, independent, and adventurous. You're also competitive and strong-willed, and you speak strongly about your views and opinions. You tend to take charge and are comfortable making swift judgments (99 percent of the time you're right too). Once you make up your mind, you likely don't ever change it unless presented with rock-solid facts. You like to know the parameters of a project and be in control. You take your work seriously and are dedicated to it. You accomplish more in an hour than anyone else you know.

Your weaknesses? Because you're so self-confident, you often don't think about how others view a situation. You don't fear hurting anyone else's feelings, so it's easy for you to be decisive and firm on your stance. You see the completion of projects as more important than how people are affected.

You also don't tolerate people who don't put in all their effort. That's why others might view you as not empathetic, bossy, or insensitive. Because you make snap judgments, they can see you as headstrong, arrogant, and impatient. You're used to people obeying you and doing things your way, so you tend to hammer those who don't and can be short-tempered. You're also overly attached to work, because you want to see a project through to its completion—even if your dinner is congealing on the table at home. What others don't know, though, is that underneath what looks like a domineering attitude is a fear of losing control and not being top dog.

You like to know the parameters of a project and be in control.

If your spouse is a choleric, what are the worst ways to respond to them?

- Question their judgment. (They'll take it personally.)
- Secretly sidestep their authority and do something behind their back you know they'd hate.
- Steal or sidetrack their limelight.
- Denigrate their accomplishments.
- Don't ask for their opinion on things that matter.
- Let them find out from somebody else what one of your kids has been up to.
- Laugh at them or don't take them seriously.

What are the best ways to respond?

- Let them have their way on things that don't matter one way or another. (What you're having for dinner tonight versus what you're having tomorrow night—does it really matter?)
- Appreciate their accomplishments. (Being seen as competent is important to them.)
- Respect them. (Think of their personality type as a military commander who is used to barking orders and doesn't see anything wrong with that.)
- Cooperate with their suggestions whenever possible.
- Compliment them in front of others, and do your part to highlight how competent they are to others, including your in-laws and their coworkers.
- If you need to approach them about a problem, introduce it by saying something nice.

    Try this: "You're amazing. You work so hard and get so much done that it blows me away. People tell me all the time how incredible you are. Like that recent project, where you . . . [and say a bit about it]. Wow. But I just wanted you to know how much I miss you when you're not here. Having dinner with you, even if it needs to be late, like 8:00, is so special to me. Do you think you could make 8:00 every night if I made dinner later?"

    Believe me, he'll listen. He may not always make 8:00, but you'll have that man around a lot more with that kind of approach.

Do those things and your choleric partner will always be in your court, have your back, and be immovable against any force. Cholerics are an incredible ally to have.

Melancholic: "Let's do it the right way."

If you're a *melancholic*, you never jump into any project. You think for a long time about *how* that project should be done. You analyze all potential angles and do lots of research about how others have done it—what has worked, what has not worked, and why—before you come up with your own way to proceed. After all, it's important to you that anything get done correctly. To accomplish that, you need time, a quiet space to yourself, and no intrusions into that thinking time. You're respectful and sensitive toward others who need those too.

"Predictable" is your middle name. You are the king of organization. No messy study or garage here—everything is color coded and labeled. You're even thinking of rearranging your dresser drawer so like underwear are together.

> *You think for a long time about how that project should be done. You analyze all potential angles and do lots of research.*

You're very good at setting long-range goals and working step by step to meet them. You tend to hang out with people who are more serious and love lengthy philosophical discussions.

You're faithful and loyal to your friends and family. You have high standards in just about everything and are an idealist who believes that if you just study something hard enough, you can figure it out and learn it.

Your weaknesses? Because you're so detail oriented, you spend a lot of time preparing for a project, and you obsess about messing up a step of that process. When you can't meet your own high standards, you can easily get discouraged and depressed. Because you analyze everything you and other people do, you can be seen as picky and negative. Though you have high ideals in your head, if they don't become reality you become moody and pessimistic. You're often a loner because your high standards drive others away.

You have no patience for happy, light people whom you view as superficial flitterbugs. You also get on your high horse if you see any smidgen of disorganization. Since disorganization surrounds us on the planet, you become easily stressed.

What people don't know about your obsessive organization and your study of the details is that, at your core, you're insecure. If someone intrudes on your thought processes, you hold grudges for a very, very long time. Cross a melancholic and you've got a typhoon to deal with. They can be both suspicious and blatantly revengeful . . . even if they act that way quietly.

If your spouse is a melancholic, what are the worst ways to respond to them?

- Say, "Would you just hurry up? We gotta go. You're killing me here."
- Intrude into their thinking space.
- Bug them to get a project done, even if it isn't perfect.
- Make fun of their ultra-organization.
- Point out a mistake they made.
- Tell them to stop being so moody. "It's not as bad as all that."

What are the best ways to respond?

- Appreciate their time spent on the details.
- Tell them how much you appreciate their sensitivity to you and your needs.
- Inform them long in advance of an upcoming activity, and explain any details you know.
- Only introduce one issue at a time, and don't push for an immediate response.
- Say, "You are so great at research—something I'm terrible at. I'm wondering if you could help me with . . ."

Do those things and your melancholic will spread his tail feathers like a proud peacock, strutting his best stuff and doing anything to support you.

Caysie is married to a melancholic. She laughed when she told me they dated seven years before he asked her to marry him. He wanted to do things right—to go through all the stages of getting to know each other so there was no question about their relationship's longevity. But that man is one of the sweetest, most sensitive, most thoughtful husbands I've ever seen.

Melancholics might take a while to grapple with a situation, but when they do, you can be sure that they've studied all the angles to come up with a solution that's a win-win.

Funny thing is, even though melancholics have little patience for lightweight people, they tend to marry sanguines. It is indeed true that opposites attract in relationships. Melancholics marry sanguines because those "happy people" have great social skills—something a melancholic lacks. Problem is, after they marry, the true nature of melancholics kicks in. They try to put their happy-go-lucky spouse who doesn't have an ounce of organization in their body into their own disciplined schedule.

If this describes you two as a couple, do you understand even more why you clash sometimes? And that any disagreement is not as much "personal" as it is your personalities?

Phlegmatic: "Let's do it the easy way."

If you're a *phlegmatic*, you'll tend to avoid conflict. You're the mediator, the peacemaker. You just want everybody to get along. Because you had to problem-solve between people a lot (starting with your siblings growing up), you've become a master at it. Your listening skills are superb, and you tend to come up with win-win situations for all.

The best word to describe you is *balanced*. You don't swing one way or another in your emotions, so people trust you. You're always even-keeled and patient. When anyone asks you how you are, you smile and say, "Just fine." Your BP doesn't spike easily. You're wonderfully adaptable, so you don't get perturbed even by curveballs.

"Loyalty" is your middle name. Once you're in someone's court, you're there to stay. If you're working on a project, it would take a crowbar to get you out of there . . . even if it does take you a while to get the project done because you're prone to distractions.

You're the mediator, the peacemaker. You just want everybody to get along.

You're often interrupted because you help out with anything and everything. People see you as friendly and someone to count on. You're the kind of neighbor everybody would love to have. You listen for hours to the elderly woman next door talk about her past, just because you know she's lonely.

Your weaknesses? Because you go out of your way to keep the peace and not offend others, you don't always say what you really think and feel. People sometimes interpret your calm demeanor as a "so what?" or "it doesn't really matter" attitude. They can also see you as a bit bland, because you never seem to get excited about anything. That's because you go with the flow and don't seem to have internal motivation or your own goals. You seem to live to please everybody else. When it comes to making any decisions, you waver because you don't want to cause problems. Often you don't make a decision at all. Underneath it all, you simply don't want to disappoint anyone. But by not taking a stand, you can look aimless, lazy, and indecisive.

If your spouse is a phlegmatic, what are the worst ways to respond to them?

- Start a fight on anything. They'll retreat immediately to their corner or try to change the subject. "Uh, would you like some cookies? Coffee? How about a donut?"
- Say, "What's wrong with you? Don't you care about anything?"

- Spout, "I know you like to help people, but it's about time you helped your own husband, don't you think?"
- Force them to set goals to get a project done.

All of these simply paralyze a person who doesn't want to disappoint you. So what are the best ways to respond?

- Highlight all their pleasing qualities. "When I want someone to count on, you're always here." "You're such a good listener. That makes me feel really special."
- Ask for their opinion. "I really want to know what you think about this. It's important to me as I look at our options."
- Point out their successes. "Nobody but you could have calmed her down, especially after that guy ran over the prize flowers she's grown forever in her garden. You're amazing, honey."
- Work right next to them on that project (or at least frequently check in and bring them snacks). Celebrate achievements along the way, and tell your partner how happy you are a task is getting done.

Do those and you'll see a more energetic phlegmatic who would knock down walls for you.

Sara is married to a phlegmatic. When they first married, it used to drive her crazy how much time her husband spent helping the neighbors—especially when they were in the middle of a project themselves. Their garage was a one-stop shop for anybody who needed help. A neighbor would show up to borrow a ladder, and Sam would not only let them borrow it but also carry it over for them and clean their gutters before returning back home.

Along the way, Sara started to appreciate Sam's balanced, problem-solving disposition and the way he'd made their neighborhood more of a community. Now, 10 years later, that couple is the hub of their multiethnic neighborhood. Visitors flow in and out of their home. Sara, a melancholic, has learned to flex on having her home look perfect, because she enjoys having spontaneous coffee and deep conversations with a neighborhood resident while Sam runs an errand with the spouse or assists him with a house project.

Their own garage has a few spiderwebs. They have a half-finished basement that they've been working on for years. There's a coffee stain on one of their couches. But their intimate connection as a couple is one that inspires the whole neighborhood.

·············

Are any of these personalities better than the others? No, they're just different. And different is what drew the two of you together in the first place.

Perhaps you were reading the personalities and thinking, *Hey, I'm somewhat like a choleric. Then again, I'm also a bit like a melancholic. What gives?* You're not alone. Most of the planet is right there with you. It's extremely rare that a person is 100 percent of any of those basic personalities. Rather, each of us is a unique blend of personality traits, filtered through the personal experiences that shape us.

Are any of these personalities better than the others? No, they're just different.

It's no surprise, then, that most of us are fascinated with classifying our personalities. We take Myers-Briggs tests or hop on easy-to-access websites such as 16personalities.com to learn more about why we do what we do, and why other people do what they do.

Understanding the blend of your personality and your spouse's, as well as your resulting strengths and weaknesses, is an important step in fine-tuning your intimate connection. Personality traits lead to what I call "purposive behavior," which means you will always behave in a way that works for you, serves a purpose in your life, and gets you to a desired goal.

You probably still have traits of the little boy or girl you once were. That's because, as you grow up, that way of behaving is reinforced as you learn through trial and error what works and what doesn't. Eventually it's ingrained in your daily existence to such an extent that it becomes a mantra you unconsciously live by. That mantra, then, develops your lifestyle (the subject of the next chapter). All three—personality, mantra, and lifestyle—have everything to do with how you respond to your spouse, communicate with them, and give and receive love.

If you had to complete the statement, "I only count in life when . . . " right now, what would you say?

SECRET #9

To Truly Know Your Partner, You Have to Understand Their Life Mantra

The seven "I only count in life when . . ."
lifestyles and how they influence
your loved one's responses.

Your Mantra

What's your life mantra? Did you even know you have one? All of us do, but for most of us, that mantra is subconscious. Here's an easy way to identify what yours is. How would you complete this statement: "I only count in life when . . ."?

Have your answer? Then take a look at these common responses. Is yours among them in some form?

I only count in life when . . .

- I'm noticed.
- I'm in control.

- I sacrifice what I want to make life easier for others.
- I make others happy.
- People tell me I did a good job or give me a reward.
- I give back to others what they really deserve.
- Well, I don't really count, because I can't do anything right.

Each of these responses was shaped first by personality and then by experiences that began in childhood. That's why the behavior you displayed when you were young likely resembles your behavior now, unless you underwent a traumatic experience that caused your personality and life mantra to change.

Kelly was mostly sanguine until she was physically abused by a stepfather who came onto the scene when she was 11. After that, no one could have guessed she had been a sanguine, since her personality flipped to mostly phlegmatic. The girl who had always wanted to entertain and be noticed and was happy-go-lucky now was afraid to ruffle anyone's feathers (especially her stepfather's). She lost her enthusiasm and became quiet.

Such changes show why it's important not only to understand your spouse now but to understand the little boy or little girl they were, as well as any adjustments they've needed to make along the way. Those adaptations have everything to do with the life mantra they've formed and what they think of you and your marriage.

What's Your Lifestyle?

Tucked within those "I only count in life when . . ." statements are seven distinct lifestyles. Which one sounds most like you? Which one sounds most like your spouse?

The Attention Getter

There's no chance at all that the attention getter is an endangered species. Fact is, there are millions of them. You or your partner may be one of them, or perhaps even both of you are.

This lifestyle is found mainly in two birth orders in the family—the firstborn and the baby. But there's a distinct difference between the two. The firstborn is more likely to seek attention in a positive way, while the baby will make you pay attention with their negative antics.

The first child of any family tends to become an attention getter because his parents' eyes are always on him. After all, he's the first child and may be the first grandchild. Every kind of attention is showered upon him the instant he's born. He cries, and Mama rushes over. He does a doodie in his diaper, and Dad (holding his nose) swiftly changes it. Every move he makes is in the spotlight of the parental eye. It's no wonder, then, that many firstborns figure out early in life, *Ah, I see. I'm the center of this universe, huh? Well, I can work that.*

So the parental guinea pig does some experimentation of his own. He sits in his high chair and frowns at the concoction on the spoon in front of him.

"Open up wide," Mom says. "Here come the rutabagas. They're good. Just try some."

He clamps his mouth shut. He wants no part of it.

Mom sighs. She hands the spoon to Dad. "You try. It's good for him. Everything I've read says it is."

> *Many firstborns figure out early in life,* **Ah, I see. I'm the center of this universe, huh? Well, I can work that.**

Dad nods. "Sure, I'll try." He picks up the spoon with the unrecognizable mushy stuff and wiggles it around like an inbound airplane in front of his son. "Here it comes, in for a landing. Gotta open the hangar for the plane," he coos.

Junior is smarter than that. His mouth stays shut.

Dad tries a new tactic. He refills the spoon and hands it to his son. "Here, you try it yourself."

Now is that boy's chance. He eyes the spoon, grabs it, and . . . *voila!* The spoon launches across the room, splattering the floor, Mom, and Dad.

His dad's response? He's not even upset. He's impressed. "Whoa, did you see how far our kid threw that thing? What an arm! I bet he's going to be another quarterback like Aaron Rodgers!"

Mom giggles.

That child, seeing the adults' reaction, will watch his dad put the spoon back on the high chair and fill it with more strained rutabagas. As soon as he has the spoon in hand, he'll throw it again, this time giggling.

Now that's a bright boy. He learns quickly. And who do you think he learned that technique from?

Dad continues to be impressed with his boy's "strong arm," smiling and laughing about it, essentially praising the child for his bad behavior. About the thirteenth time Junior throws the spoon, though, Dad starts to get irritated.

However, the damage has been done. Dad's initial laughter already caused his son to understand exactly how he can get attention and play enjoyable games with an adult—by displaying this behavior.

Fast-forward another couple of years, and let a middleborn dare to try this same trick. He's likely to get an immediate lecture about being naughty. He might even be marooned in that high chair in the next room, spoon-less and rutabaga-less, while his family finishes dinner.

Dad and Mom are no longer newbies at parenting. They've seen this kind of thing before and aren't interested in seeing it again. Their fuses are shorter now that they have two kids to watch.

The middleborn learns quickly that the best thing to do is stay out of Mom and Dad's reach and sight. No wonder that child becomes secretive and has the easiest time slipping away from dinner unnoticed.

That's only one example of the way children learn early in life that they can do things to command their parents' attention. Attention can quickly become its own reward—whether it's positive or negative.

Firstborns are more likely to seek attention in a positive, *constructive* way. They already walk and talk more quickly than their siblings, largely because their parents work with them and dialogue with them more.

When a firstborn goes off to school, he tends to do very well—again, largely because this is the first go-round for Mom and Dad, and they're attentive to his homework and interacting with the teachers. At school he also gets attention for being the "cream of the crop" who does what he's told, works hard, and gets top grades. He learns how to read quickly. He's usually good with numbers.

Then there's the lastborn, who usually gets attention because of his *destructive* antics that keep Mom and Dad on their toes. However, a baby-of-the-family attention getter doesn't really care what *kind* of attention he gets—he simply wants to be at the center of it. That means he'll do anything he can to get others to take notice. He'll cut off the ponytail of the girl who sits in front of him. He'll shave half of the prized family cat. He'll crawl out of class when he gets bored with it while the teacher's back is turned. He'll launch day-old jelly donuts at passing cars.

The person who seeks attention in a negative way will indeed try nearly anything . . . once.

I should know, since I'm a lastborn and was the clown—sometimes the not-so-funny one—of my family. I've done at least one of the antics in the paragraph above. I'll let you figure out which one(s).

I know all about negative attention. My mama, May Leman, truly was a saint (she was a phlegmatic all the way) and the reason I lived through my childhood. My life could have been over numerous times with all my antics, but she always believed in me and had my back.

The person who seeks attention in a negative way will indeed try nearly anything . . . once.

One set of parents showed up in my counseling office because their little boy was eating pencils.

"Why are you eating pencils?" I asked him plainly.

"I don't know," he mumbled.

"You don't know?" I said. "Do you *like* pencils?"

He shrugged. "I guess so."

But what that kid really wanted was plenty of attention, and he got it. Word was all over the school. I mean, he was almost famous, as in, "Hey, are you that kid who eats pencils?"

Sure, he got funny looks at times, like he was a bit crazy. But at least people looked at him, and that's what he wanted. His life mantra was, "I only count when I get people's attention and they notice me."

If the only time a child gets the attention he craves from his parents is when he misbehaves, you can be certain he'll misbehave more and more frequently.

These days, that kid is a grown-up. I wonder what he's eating now. Does he get attention at the office by chowing down on a USB drive? What in the world does he pack in his lunch? Or does he no longer need roughage?

A certain amount of attention-getting behavior in and of itself is not a bad thing. We're all human. We like to be noticed. Seeking attention can spur a child on to the heights of achievement, as it often does for firstborns. But for them, it also brings a lot of pressure as they try to maintain that height of achievement in everything they do.

An inordinate need for attention is never healthy, especially when it enters the realm of an adult relationship. What happened to Joel and Suzi is a good example.

An inordinate need for attention is never healthy.

Suzi was the little princess of her family. Not only was she the youngest, but she was also the only girl among four boys. This apple of her daddy's eye was precocious, demanding, and very good at getting others to notice her. She used her charm, cuteness, and temper—complete with stomping foot and dramatic flair—to demand attention.

She had all her brothers wrapped around that little princess pinkie finger.

Joel had grown up as the man of the house because his father had died when Joel was only nine. He was reliable, conscientious, and perfectionistic. He was convinced that he knew what was best for everyone, including Suzi.

Joel was also a bicycling enthusiast who liked to go on "little" biking trips of, say, 40 to 50 miles. He approached this hobby the way he did everything else in his life—full throttle. He wanted to go faster. He wanted to go farther. He wanted to have more muscle and greater breathing capacity. He wanted to accomplish and achieve. If you saw him, you'd think he was training for the Tour de France. And he "knew" Suzi would love those trips too, so he invested a good $700 in a racing bike for her . . . without consulting her first.

To her credit, his unathletic wife gave that racing bike a pretty good try before she decided that such an activity simply wasn't for her. She couldn't keep up with him, and she didn't particularly enjoy chasing him down some country road and watching the distance between them grow.

When she decided she'd had enough of that particular sport, she told him she was staying home.

He shrugged. "Okay," he said, and that was that. No further discussion. For the next several weekends he left her at home while he rode off on his own . . . and was gone most of their free time.

Suzi became angrier and angrier. She wanted the attention that her husband was giving to that "stupid" bike.

One Sunday afternoon Joel returned sweaty and exhausted after nearly a whole day of bicycling. Immediately he flopped down in front of the TV, ignoring Suzi.

That was the last straw for her. She decided to voice her anger in a most definite way.

Joel's only other pride in life besides that bike was his prize bed of tulips. It was about forty feet long and four feet wide, with beautiful flowers in a perfectly positioned array of colors. At least, it was before Suzi took the trimming shears to it. By the time she was through, not a flower was left. Nothing but stems looking like a bunch of oversized toothpicks pointing toward the sky.

Yes, that act got Suzi some attention from Joel. It wasn't particularly *good* attention—I'm sure she also had some neighbors wondering what was going on—but it was attention nonetheless. Mission accomplished.

That's when they came to see me.

After a few sessions, both were able to see why such an event occurred. Suzi's need for attention and Joel's need to achieve were both driving forces in their lives, and they'd clashed. To get their relationship on a healthy footing, both needed to work on modifying their behavior. That meant becoming aware of each other's needs and personalities.

Joel soon learned that every time he put his wife in a position where she was the center of attention, she purred like a kitten. Suzi learned to give Joel credit for his achievements and realized that occasionally he needed to have time by himself, with that bike, to regroup.

Meanwhile, Joel agreed to budget his time more equally, also doing some activities Suzi liked. They agreed on set hours for Joel to take off and do his cycling. Occasionally Suzi even joined him, but they rode gently, side by side, instead of in racing fashion. Sometimes they even took along a roadside picnic.

If you only pay attention to your spouse when she does something wrong, she'll continue to do things she knows you hate— nagging, spending too much money, being late to your parents' house for dinner, even cutting off your prize tulips—because that's the only way she's guaranteed that you'll look at her and address her. How much better it would be to get on the front end—paying attention to your spouse for the positive things she does.

Saying "thank you" has never gone out of style. Make sure it's in your vocabulary with your loved one on a daily basis.

The Controller

The controlling lifestyle is among the most difficult to deal with, especially within a marriage. The controller tends to play his cards very close to his chest, only rarely giving his partner a glimpse of his real self. I use "his" because controllers are usually a specific rank and gender—firstborn males.

There are basically two types of controllers. One controls because he enjoys pulling all the strings and being in charge of every situation. The other controls for defensive purposes. He's afraid that someone else may take him down a path he doesn't want to go.

But underneath both types of control is fear. The controller is afraid. He's afraid he'll die. He's afraid he'll lose his mind. He's afraid others will betray him. That's why he'd much prefer to stay locked in that protective shell, even though it keeps at bay the person who loves him the most—you.

Kurt was a controller who expressed his need to be in charge through perfectionism and an overemphasis on neatness. Not surprisingly, he was an accountant, a profession where his perfectionistic tendencies were useful and helped get him promoted. But his perfectionism and standoffishness were greatly hurting his relationship with Linda, his wife, and halting any potential for an intimate connection.

Kurt was, in every definition of the term, a bean counter—both on and off the job. He was always busy with his figurative stack of beans, counting each one over and over, making sure none of them got spilled or lost. Every time Linda wanted to talk to him or cuddle with him, he was busy. He always found something to do, such as washing the car or fixing something in their apartment.

"It's like he actually *avoids* me," she complained, "except on the nights he wants something . . . and you know what I mean."

On those nights he'd pursue her in a very methodical, clinical manner, without any overt consideration of her desires or even any affection for her. It seemed like something he did just so he could check it off his list.

Understandably, Linda didn't react well to his overtures. There was no affection, no love talk . . . until he decided he wanted to do the wild thing. No wonder she felt angry and used.

Linda had come to see me because Kurt didn't think they had a problem. Well, they did. A significant mountain of a problem. She was trying to change him into something he wasn't. It was like trying to turn a hyena into a leopard just by adding spots.

For 13 years of marriage, she'd pleaded, coaxed, and reminded him that affection was important to her. Nothing had worked.

She was trying to change him into something he wasn't. It was like trying to turn a hyena into a leopard just by adding spots.

I finally convinced her that the only way for change to happen was for her to act in a completely different manner than she had before. She had to back off and give up trying to remake him into what he wasn't.

When she no longer nagged and pursued him but went about her own business, Kurt was at first confused. He sensed something was changing in their relationship, but he didn't know why.

Soon, however, he realized his wife was no longer under his thumb. He felt a bit threatened by her independence. Finally he sought her out and hesitantly asked a few questions.

"Uh, is something wrong?"

No response. She simply continued the task she was doing in the kitchen as if she hadn't even heard him.

"Do we need to talk about something?"

Again, no response.

"Did *I* do something wrong?"

Those were wonderful words to Linda's ears, and she swiveled to face him with a calm countenance. Kurt was finally ready to listen to what she needed to say.

Those words also got Kurt to come with Linda to my office.

After several sessions, he admitted that he'd always been afraid. "If I tell Linda who I really am, what I'm like on the inside, and how inadequate I feel . . . and guilty for the way I treat the person I love so much . . . then she'll reject me."

He'd been taught in his home that the man was "the strong one" and that sharing any feelings was displaying weakness. So he'd shut his feelings off.

Months later, their marriage had transformed. Both told me about the highlight of their now 14-year marriage—the night they wept in each other's arms for the first time.

Is it always easy for Kurt to share with his wife now? No, sometimes he slides back to his learned behavior of shutting her out. He has to consciously process through this pattern of thinking:

Am I doing what I used to do?

Well, yes, I am.

Did it work before?

No, and it hurt Linda. So I shouldn't do it again. I need to do things differently.

This is "calling an audible at the line of scrimmage," to use football terminology. The offensive unit will go into a huddle to decide what play they're going to run. But occasionally, when the team lines up to begin the play, the quarterback will notice that the defensive unit has anticipated his play selection. For those of you who don't understand football, that means the defense is lined up in such a way that they are certain to stop the play he's selected. That's when he calls an audible—a number sequence that lets his teammates know to go to a different play.

Because Kurt knows that his tendency is to be closed and controlled—to shut his wife out when she comes to him looking for affection—he can call an audible and refuse to give in to that learned behavior. Now when his wife wants to talk to him, he may not feel like it at the moment, but he can still tell himself, *It's important to Linda that she talk to me. It will help her if I share what's on my mind, or even simply listen. So even though I don't feel like doing that right now, I'll do it because I love her, and that meets her need to be loved.*

Feelings will come and go, but you don't have to give in to them. There's always plenty of time to call an audible at the line of scrimmage.

It didn't surprise me when Kurt also told me he was very shy as a child. Shyness is one factor that can be used to control the behavior of others. Not every controller comes in a loud package. Sometimes whispers can be used to control people.

Feelings will come and go, but you don't have to give in to them.

I once worked with a five-year-old girl who talked in a sweet, gentle voice you could barely hear. As she sat in the chair in my office, her short legs dangling in the air, I had to inch closer to her to understand what she was saying.

Then it hit me. (I am a psychologist, after all.) That little girl had me in the palm of her hand. I could almost hear the wheels turning in her head and could see what she was thinking. *In another minute or two, I'll get this crazy psychologist to fall off his chair and onto the floor, flat on his face. Won't that be funny?*

When I leaned back in my chair and stopped playing the game with her, it was amazing how loud her voice became.

You see, recognizing a controller isn't always easy. Some of them can hide in plain sight. Your quiet partner might be the last person you'd suspect of being interested in controlling others. But when she approaches you from a position of shyness, she's actually saying, "Pay attention to me. If you don't, I'm going to demand that you do. I *will* control this situation."

Controllers can come in nearly polar-opposite packages. They may use a nasty temper, a flood of tears, shyness, and even intellectualizing to keep people at a distance. But their life mantra is all based on a power principle: "I only count in life when I'm in control." It's a "my way or the highway" view of life.

What can you do if you're married to a controller? Refuse to give in to their controlling behavior. A marriage isn't a dictatorship. It's a democracy, with everybody giving and getting equally. It's about two people working together for their mutual satisfaction—not one person getting his way.

Not every controller comes in a loud package. Sometimes whispers can be used to control people.

You're half of this relationship, right? Then act like it. Don't let your spouse get away with controlling you.

The Martyr

Martyrs don't think they're worthy—of anything. They're also experts at making people feel guilty or uncomfortable.

If you came upon an accident in which a martyr's leg was severely damaged, they'd probably say, "Oh, don't worry about me. I'm sure I can get along. Why don't you see about that poor guy over there? I think he's got a broken fingernail. You go on. Yes, I'm in excruciating pain, but I'll be fine."

See what I mean? So how does this translate to relationships in the real world?

Martyrs are the most difficult personality type to deal with, frankly, because they have the need to do themselves harm and are always putting themselves in unenviable positions. They are perfectly capable of giving but haven't the slightest idea how to take. It's a foreign concept to them. Yet for any relationship to be healthy, there needs to be a fair amount of give-and-take.

In my experience, a martyr is very likely to be married to an alcoholic. An alcoholic needs a martyr to use, and martyrs have the deplorable need to be walked on. Or a martyr may be married to an abuser—or a person who is both an alcoholic *and* an abuser. That's because, early in life, martyrs develop the feeling that they're not worth loving. They tend to have a poor relationship with the opposite-sex parent, who treats them badly. But then, as soon as they are free of that parent, they choose a life partner who reinforces their negative feelings about themselves.

When James came to my office, he explained that he was there because of the terrible panic attacks he had in supermarkets. He was agoraphobic, meaning he was afraid of being in open spaces, and would get to the point where he'd have to run from the store because he felt like his air supply was being cut off and he was about to pass out.

He hadn't yet told me very much about his marriage, except that he'd recently gotten married for the second time. So imagine his shock when I said, "James, I'll bet you anything your wife is an alcoholic."

He stared at me. "She is, but how did you know?"

"I didn't know, but I guessed, because you just told me you're a martyr. You had to run out of the store for fear someone would see you faint."

You see, I was hearing that James didn't believe he was worth the attention he'd get if he passed out in the store.

John and Alice, another couple, had a martyr living with them—Alice's mom. That cranky older lady was doing a good job of making her daughter and son-in-law feel guilty if they went anywhere and left her home alone.

"I might just die while you're off gallivanting around," she'd say in a weary monotone every time they went out the door.

Alice couldn't count the number of times they'd turned back around, changed their plans, and stayed home. They were going out of their way to be ever sensitive to Mom's needs—she was getting up there in years, after all. But their marriage was fraying around the edges as a result. With someone always between them as a couple, there was no whisper of a chance for an intimate connection.

It was only when they made a commitment to take care of their own relationship first—spending time away and solely with each other—that Mom's martyr-like behavior began to decrease. That behavior only works if others accept the martyr's "sacrifice" on their behalf.

Alice's mom had a long history of martyr behavior, since her husband had grown more and more abusive throughout their marriage. She had at last left him after Alice got married. But her martyr-like pattern had continued in Alice's home once she moved in.

When her daughter and son-in-law no longer accepted that martyr lifestyle, interestingly, she actually discovered some new hobbies to enjoy when she had time by herself. One was baking, and Alice and John were delighted to share in the results.

When I think of a martyr, I think of someone who is married to an abusive spouse but refuses to leave to protect himself or herself. Or someone who enables an alcoholic partner to continue in their destructive lifestyle by making excuses for them or covering up for them, saying, "If I only love that person enough, everything will work out okay."

I admire those who love their sick partners, want to help them, and stand by them even when their behavior is completely unlovable. However, only up to a point. If the abusive partner refuses to get professional help to deal with their hostility, I believe the other partner has no choice but to leave. No one deserves to be yelled at, struck, or beaten . . . not even the neighborhood stray dog. And neither do you.

If the alcoholic will not take steps to overcome their addiction, I believe the other partner needs to exit that marriage. Nothing good will come of staying and being a part of the downward spiral, since it's inevitable without professional assistance.

Early in life, martyrs develop the feeling that they're not worth loving.

Most martyrs are married to extreme controllers. If this is you, leaving a situation that's degrading to you is to be applauded. It's hard to take such a step, especially if it's the first positive step you've taken in your life to protect yourself. However, doing so reaffirms the fact that you are a human being worth loving. If you've been stepped on and squashed over a long period of time, it's very difficult to get to the point where you can gain some notion of self-esteem or respect, but it can and must be done.

If you find that you are a martyr, it's time to look yourself in the mirror and say, "I am worthy of love. I am worthy of respect. I am worthy of being treated well."

Don't stay in a relationship that reinforces your negative view of yourself. If your partner isn't willing to get help, it's time for you to get out of that relationship.

If you find that you are a martyr, it's time to look yourself in the mirror and say, "I *am* worthy of love. I *am* worthy of respect. I *am* worthy of being treated well." Then you need to do something nice for yourself. Buy yourself a new shirt or take an evening to do an activity you'd enjoy—relax with a good book, take a long shower, attend a concert. It won't be easy for you to do something that feels terribly indulgent—after all, it's just for *you.* But go ahead, take that small step. Then take another, and another. Major changes in the martyr lifestyle can happen by taking just one small step at a time.

Most of all, remember that none of us are carpets to be walked on. We're human beings worthy of being loved, worthy of standing up for ourselves, able to give and to take. There's no relationship without mutual satisfaction or caring intimately for each other's needs in a healthy manner. That's the message a martyr needs to hear and begin to act on.

The Pleaser

Pleasers, like controllers, are usually a specific rank and gender—firstborn females. They tend to go with the flow and don't express their honest opinions because they want to please everyone and want all to be happy.

My wife, Sande, has some tendencies of a pleaser, and those came into play one night when we were having dinner in a nice restaurant. Sande had ordered salmon, but when it arrived at our table, it looked as if it still had a fighting chance of getting upstream to spawn.

"Oh, it's not quite done," Sande said quietly, but she began eating around the more fully cooked edges.

No way am I going to pay for that! I thought. So I called the waiter over, told him my lady's salmon wasn't done, and asked him to please return it to the kitchen.

The waiter was most apologetic and quickly took her plate away.

Moments later the maître d' came to our table and expressed his sincere apologies. Two minutes later the headwaiter came over, relaying the chef's apologies and bringing the news that the chef was preparing a little something for dessert, compliments of the house, as his way of showing how sorry he was for not having the dinner prepared correctly.

Within a few minutes, a new salmon was back on the table, done to perfection. And when we were finished, the waiter brought us baked Alaska flambé, covered with a pure marshmallow sauce and drenched with fresh strawberries.

With that kind of treatment, we've returned to that restaurant often. And every time we go, I complain about the way my meal is cooked in hopes of getting another terrific dessert. (I'm kidding, of course, but I'd do almost anything for that baked Alaska. It was incredibly delicious.) If I hadn't said something initially, my lovely bride would not have said anything and would have picked her way carefully around the very edges of that meal.

How do you know if you're a pleaser? Think about that situation. If you are served a restaurant meal that isn't to your liking, what would you do? Would you send it back to the kitchen or just try to eat it, even if it's nearly raw or not what you ordered?

If you're a pleaser, you'll usually just eat it because you don't want to make waves. You'll even leave your regular tip to boot. You don't want to do anything that causes friction because you don't want others to be upset, especially with you.

In many cases, pleasers are firstborn attention getters who learned early in life that the best way to win approval is not to make waves. "Go along to get along" is their life mantra.

If you are served a restaurant meal that isn't to your liking, what would you do? Would you send it back to the kitchen or just try to eat it, even if it's nearly raw or not what you ordered?

That works for a while. But then one day that pleaser starts to think, *Hey, what about me? What about my needs? Am I the only one who doesn't count here? When is someone going to meet my needs?*

Have you ever heard one of those stories where a spouse suddenly hightailed it somewhere else, and no one could figure out why?

"I don't understand it," a frazzled husband says. "How could she run off to Mexico like that and leave me and the kids? It just doesn't seem like her."

That may seem like a drastic situation, but it does happen. However, what happens more frequently is that the feeling of getting used grows and grows under the surface until there's an explosion.

All too often, a husband is more than happy to take advantage of his pleaser wife's lifestyle instead of doing his best to help her overcome it and take some time for herself along the way. He's content to watch her rush around with a plastic smile, doing everything she can for him and others. He doesn't often notice that behind that fake smile is someone becoming angrier and angrier at him . . . until the explosion happens.

The most important thing you can do for a pleaser partner is to open the doors of communication by saying things like, "Honey, I'd like to know what you want to do in this situation. Please tell me what you'd *really* like—not what you're supposed to say or think I want to hear. What you think and how you feel are very important to me because you're my wife and I love you."

Those words not only open the communication doors but also give a pleaser something else she needs: your approval. You see, pleasers want everybody everywhere to approve of everything they do. But the one who matters most to her is you.

There are always people who are ready to take advantage of pleasers for their "agreeable" attitude.

The pleaser woman may be in a carpool with four other women, all of whom are supposed to drive the kids to school one day a week. Instead, she finds herself driving at least two days, and sometimes as many as three, even though she also works a part-time job. That's because whenever one of the other women wants a break, she knows the pleaser won't say no to the question, "Will you please drive for me today?"

The pleaser man (yes, there are some, but the number is far fewer than women) may refuse to stand up in defense of his family because he doesn't want to make waves. Let's say his son comes home from a neighborhood baseball game and says that Billy hit the ball through Mrs. Smith's window. But Billy lied and said he did it. So now Mrs. Smith is angry and will soon be on the pleaser's doorstep to insist his son pay for it.

Will the pleaser back up his son? Will he march over to Billy's father and tell the truth, then do the same with Mrs. Smith?

No, when that angry woman shows up, the pleaser is likely to say, "I'm so sorry your window is broken. Don't worry about it. I'll just pay for it."

He doesn't want to make waves with anyone, nor does he want to create hard feelings. But what he's really done is undercut his son and their relationship by not standing up for him.

Pleasers have a hard time disciplining their kids because they want their kids to love them. "If I ground her for the weekend, she might get mad at me!"

Yes, she likely will, but maybe that kid will learn something if she has to sit in her room at home instead of going out with her girlfriends.

In the same way, pleaser partners don't want to upset their spouse. However, there are times in life where they simply have to do what's right and run the risk of making other people angry.

If you're a pleaser, it's time to make some changes for your own sake, before you exhaust yourself and grow angrier under the surface. So do this. Stand in front of the mirror and practice saying a two-letter word: NO. Say it so many times it becomes ingrained in your vocabulary.

Stand in front of the mirror and practice saying a two-letter word: NO. Say it so many times it becomes ingrained in your vocabulary.

The next time someone—even your spouse—asks you to do something you don't want to do, form your lips into that little round shape and just say no.

Practice saying no as often as you can, or expressing your honest opinion whenever you are given the opportunity. It will be hard to say no the first few times you try it. You may find yourself getting dizzy and your palms starting to sweat. But as you continue to use that technique, before long you'll be standing up for yourself with only a modest amount of effort.

If you're married to a pleaser, stand up for them at every opportunity, just as I did in the restaurant with Sande. I knew she didn't want to eat that half-cooked salmon. I mean, would you? But it wasn't within her pleaser nature to complain about it.

One of the perks of having a partner is that you're in the game of life together, and you should support each other on that playing board. You need to be strong where your partner is weak, and vice versa. So even as you encourage your pleaser to tell you more how she feels, you also need to do some mind reading—*Ah, I see that she's not happy about this*—and then act according to her best interests.

You can also encourage your pleaser to begin to speak up on her own behalf. Role-model through your own actions that sticking up for yourself doesn't have to be done in an obnoxious or rude way. She can say no nicely and still get the job done. And saying no can and does bring tremendous benefits to her life, like having time for a cup of tea all by herself instead of running around in that carpool . . . or eating salmon that could still live if thrown back in the water.

The Carrot Seeker

When you did something good at home, were you rewarded in some way? When you did something bad, were you punished?

If so, then you've grown up with the traditional view of reward and punishment. Many of us have, and that's why so many of us still look for a reward for everything we do in life. We also fear punishment if we don't do what we feel we're supposed to. Remember your childhood, when it seemed that your mom or dad had X-ray, 360-degree vision and could catch you at anything you did wrong? Such memories are ingrained.

The carrot seeker grew up with a strong experience of reward and punishment. So even now, as an adult, he goes around looking for a carrot at every turn. When he doesn't receive praise or reinforcement from his partner for every little achievement, he's deeply offended and hurt.

Very similar to the pleaser lifestyle, the carrot seeker says, "I only count in life when other people notice what I do and reward me for such behavior."

> *The carrot seeker says, "I only count in life when other people notice what I do and reward me for such behavior."*

Then the real world hits, and that lifestyle generally becomes unfulfilling. Receiving a "thank you" for everything you do or expecting some mention of approval simply isn't realistic, nor is it healthy. That's because when a carrot seeker is doing things for others, he's really doing them for *himself*—to be noticed and rewarded.

If you spend four hours preparing a gourmet dinner and your partner gobbles it down in a few minutes, then leaves the table without telling you how great it was, wouldn't you be hurt?

If you spend a month preparing a surprise for your spouse—one you know she'll like—but she just takes a look, says, "How nice," and walks away, would you feel slighted with only that much appreciation and recognition?

If so, you're likely to have carrot-seeking tendencies.

The full carrot seeker, though, is a bit different. That is the person who volunteers for every single committee or for overtime at work for the simple reason that he wants to be praised and recognized for all his hard work. If both partners are carrot seekers, they may try to outdo each other in doing good things for each other, but that's only because each has a need to get praise from their spouse.

Becky and Steve came to see me because they had an interesting problem. The husband was always outdoing the wife when it came to housework. Now there's a switch. Problem was, he wouldn't let up. If all the work was caught up, he'd wash the windows or tackle the bathroom tile with a toothbrush.

Becky, to her credit, was no slouch when it came to keeping up with things. Yet sometimes she'd find herself saying, "Come on, honey, let's go out for some coffee. I'll take care of that tomorrow."

His response was invariably, "Oh, no, I'll do it now. I don't want you to have to worry about it."

As we talked, he at last came to see that his total motivation in working so hard was winning praise from his wife. He wanted her to tell her friends, "My husband's the greatest! You won't believe all the work he does for me."

He wanted her to praise and thank him 24 hours a day. Instead, he was driving her crazy. She resented him because she felt he was trying to show her up. It made her seem lazy, and she didn't like it, especially because she was a detailed firstborn with a high sense of responsibility.

You see why these two clashed?

But I give them lots of credit. First, they reached out for some help. And second, when they realized what was prompting their behaviors, both made a conscious effort to change. Now they do have time for that cup of coffee, and they have a much more intimate connection because they've carved out some time for communicating their hearts.

If you are a carrot seeker, you and the martyr have something in common. You both need to do something for yourself at least once a week. Maybe you walk around the block listening to good music in your earbuds, read a book a week, take a class at the local community college, or play tennis at the park with whoever happens to be there that day. Just make sure it's only for *your* personal satisfaction.

When others decide to thank you for something, that should be a fun bonus, not a requirement for you to feel good about yourself.

What's the reward? You're doing things that feel worthwhile, yet other people won't be thanking you for it. You really don't need the approval and praise of everyone else—only your own feelings of self-worth. When others decide to thank you for something, that should be a fun bonus, not a requirement for you to feel good about yourself.

It's not only okay but good for you to treat yourself well just because you're worth it.

The Cop-Out Artist

The person with a cop-out lifestyle is generally either an oldest child or a youngest child.

If he's the firstborn, chances are his parents had very high expectations for him. They were also critical, so he feared not meeting those nearly impossible expectations. It's like a kid looking up at the high bars on a playground, knowing he can never jump high enough to reach them.

If he's the youngest in his family, chances are good the siblings above him were very successful, which defeated him before he could even begin to achieve. After all, who can compete with the family stars—the volleyball captain, the Little League star pitcher, the straight-A student, the first-chair trombonist?

Cop-outs become inadequate, primarily because that's the way they see themselves. Rarely do you see these people complete any kind of task. And when they grow older, it's abnormal for them to even start tasks. Their mission seems to be to prove to others that they can't do anything efficiently or correctly.

Cop-outs become inadequate, primarily because that's the way they see themselves.

Cop-out artists will look helpless and incapable, but they're far from it. They've just adopted a lifestyle that makes them appear that way in order to protect themselves. When they couldn't keep up with their star siblings, they just gave up. "Better not to try anything than to try it and fail" is their life mantra.

If your spouse simply floats through life, not seeming to have much enthusiasm for anything, and is reticent to try anything new, he's likely a cop-out artist. In that case, if you want to help him, you'll have to do some things that are likely hard for you to do, because you love him.

Truth is, it's very difficult for cop-out artists to help themselves. If something is to be done to change their lifestyle and the way they think about themselves, it has to be done by another person. To help cop-out artists, the people closest to them have to withdraw from the scene, refusing to do something for them that they can or should do for themselves.

Let's say your spouse needs to mail a USPS package. He says, "Well, I've never done that before, so I don't know how to do it."

You don't rescue him. You say simply, "I know you can figure that out. See you tonight, honey," and you walk out the door without looking back.

So either he steps up to the plate and checks out the easy USPS Click-N-Ship online, figuring out how to wrap that package and get it to your mailbox on time, or that package he wanted to get somewhere will still be sitting in your living room when you get home.

It's very difficult for cop-out artists to help themselves. If something is to be done to change their lifestyle and the way they think about themselves, it has to be done by another person.

Either way, it's not your responsibility. Don't do his responsibilities for him, or he'll never change.

The cop-out artist is likely to need some professional help. There's a lot of baggage in his background. Multiple factors caused him to adopt this lifestyle. He's afraid not only to fail but to fail even if he gives his best effort. He's terrified at his core to try anything. He knows his efforts will amount to nothing, because he could never please his parents or jump high enough over their hurdles when he was a kid.

He'll also be too afraid to try any changes in your relationship because he just *knows* anything he does is programmed to fail. In such a situation, with only one of you doing the work, there's no possibility of gaining an intimate connection.

That's why you need to get that cop-out artist some professional help—for his sake and for the sake of anyone who loves him.

The Revenger

The revengeful lifestyle takes some time to develop, but it usually is fairly strongly entrenched in the revenger personality by the time a child is eight or nine. In this lifestyle, the mantra is, "Life has treated me unfairly, so I have a right to strike back in any way I can."

Anything that happens negatively in this person's life from that point on only reinforces in his mind how unfair life is to him and escalates a desire for revenge. This revengeful lifestyle often manifests itself in violence—domestic violence, school shootings, etc.

It's not very often that revengers can even admit they need help. That's because they lack trust in anyone and feel that they'll only be hurt. But on rare occasions I've worked with them.

In this lifestyle, the mantra is, "Life has treated me unfairly, so I have a right to strike back in any way I can."

In one counseling session it was Roger, the husband, who came to see me because he was deeply concerned about his wife's behavior. Marion had grown up in a home where her father had abused her and her mother before deserting the family when she was only six. Though she'd had a rough start in life, she worked hard, becoming such a good student that she got numerous scholarships—enough to finish college and graduate school with a degree in psychology.

Three years earlier, a baby had joined their family through adoption. He was the delight of their lives. But the previous week Roger had returned home from work to find their three-year-old cowering in the corner and covered with bruises. Marion was nowhere in sight.

Roger was stunned. He'd thought a couple of times earlier that she seemed to be verbally harsh with the boy when he did something wrong, but this was his first indication that his wife had become physically abusive.

Sad to say, Marion was simply following the parenting patterns she'd experienced while growing up. When something went wrong, she reacted the same way her father had—hitting the offending child. Ironically, she'd been trained in psychology but couldn't identify how her own background had prompted such behavior.

I wish I could say that story had a happy ending, but it didn't. Marion refused any help. The only positive thing that came out of professional help was that Roger and their three-year-old left that day to live in a different apartment, since the boy's safety was the top priority. Eventually, Roger also parted ways with Marion, who seemed determined to vent her frustration and anger in a violent manner.

Both father and son went through a series of counseling sessions. Roger wanted to make sure his son knew that the situation was not normal, and that little boys should not expect to be hurt by their mommies. Today Roger and his son are doing well and have a close father-son relationship. They haven't heard from Marion or anything about her in over eight years.

Is it possible for someone like Marion to change her behavior? Yes, it's possible. Anything's possible. But the revengeful lifestyle was so deeply entrenched in her personality that change is extremely unlikely. Yet I've seen a marvelous transformation happen in the life of another couple where the husband was the revenger.

Melody contacted me because of Jerry's verbal outbursts. He was a millionaire who owned property all over the world, a nationally known expert in his field, and a man greatly respected by his peers. He had everything a man could want, including a beautiful, charming, and competent wife. Yet he was an angry man. Melody was the frequent recipient of his violent temper and booming voice.

Many times she was so shaken by his outbursts in public that she ran from the room in tears. She'd developed migraines and gastrointestinal problems because she was constantly uptight. Stress was consuming her energy and keeping her from being productive.

Jerry finally agreed to come see me when his wife ended up in the hospital.

My first task was to find out what had made him a revenger. When I asked him to describe his earliest memories of life, he couldn't go back any farther than the time he was 16 years old. That's most unusual, so I queried him about it. Eventually his story came out in broken bits and pieces.

At age 16, Jerry remembered hearing a gunshot. When he ran into the next room to see what was going on, his father was holding a gun to his head. He had killed his wife and then proceeded to take his own life in front of his son.

That same day Jerry's older sister, unable to handle the trauma, also killed herself.

Jerry's response was to pull down a steel curtain on his life and memories that would block out the time. Until he met with me for a series of sessions, he was unable to go back and remember anything before that age.

In his mind, he had a right to be angry and bitter. Who wouldn't feel that way after suffering through something like that? It's no wonder he developed a revenger lifestyle.

As a young man alone, he'd developed a tremendous amount of independence. He closed others out of his life, feeling that he'd have to make it on his own, since he was the lone survivor of his family.

When he married Melody and they began to work side by side in the business, he developed what he thought was a nasty habit that came out of nowhere. He would all of a sudden viciously explode verbally at her.

When I asked what precipitated those outbursts, neither of them could give a definitive answer.

"Something inside me just snaps, and I blow up," Jerry finally managed.

I asked Melody to write down the words they spoke to each other just before an explosion, and something fascinating emerged that I had already guessed was there. The key word that set Jerry off was *why*. Whenever Melody asked why, he felt she was challenging his authority and knowledge.

The miraculous transformation in their relationship started with eliminating the word *why* from Melody's vocabulary. The outbursts reduced by 75 percent in just the first two weeks. Both Jerry and Melody were stunned by the change. They were even smiling when they came to see me next. And in therapy Jerry felt for the first time that he had "permission" to talk about his feelings—especially his anger and need to exact revenge.

Something even more wonderful occurred along the way. Their connection became more intimate as Jerry opened up to Melody. Even though he'd always tried to repel anyone who attempted to get close to him, as a human being he still had an urgent need to talk about his feelings, thoughts, and fears. But since his tragic family background wasn't known to any of his acquaintances, and all those who knew him felt they had to walk on eggshells around him, no one had ever taken the time to really get to know him. He had business colleagues but no one close enough to be his friend.

With work on both their parts, Melody and Jerry developed the kind of relationship where they could talk about anything. But without looking at his childhood and the way it determined his current behavior, they wouldn't be as warm and intimate as they are today.

What in your childhood experiences is stopping you from seeking an intimate connection with the one you love? The lifestyle you've adopted is a result of how you view the world due to prior experiences. Many of those lifestyles are founded on falsehoods. You don't have to control or dominate or get others' attention to count for something.

What in your childhood experiences is stopping you from seeking an intimate connection with the one you love?

Your experiences earlier in life are perceptions. Your feelings about those experiences, your parents, and your siblings—all taken together—have developed in you a biased perception of yourself. That perception reveals itself through predictable behavior in the lifestyle you adopt.

A negative, destructive lifestyle doesn't have to control you or your most intimate relationship for the rest of your life. It can be changed. All it takes is one step at a time and a willingness to take that step . . . like Melody and Jerry did.

Step on Stage . . . into a New Play the Two of You Create

In short, your personality, the life mantra you adopt, and the life-style you unwittingly choose as a result have everything to do with your satisfaction with your spouse and how you respond in your relationship.

You see life through your own custom-tinted lens. That lens is colored by the vast experiences you've had with fickle critters called people in your past. The happier those relationships have been, the more open you will be to seeking an intimate connection with your spouse. If you haven't experienced much hurt, you'll always see the positive before the negative in your spouse. You'll be a sunny-side-up person.

However, if your relationships have been destructive in any way, that lens will be colored with a darker filter. You'll feel like a victim, even if your spouse doesn't treat you that way. You'll exhibit martyr tendencies. You'll try to please or control others. You'll always see the negative before the positive in any action your spouse takes.

You didn't become the person you are out of thin air. You *learned* to be that person, based on real or imagined wrongs in your life.

You know these secrets, so what will you do about them? Will you keep being an attention getter? A controller? A martyr? A pleaser? A carrot seeker? A cop-out artist? A revenger? Unless you choose to act differently, you'll automatically act out what you've learned along the way.

Now's your chance. As of this moment, you and your spouse are standing on a stage, and you're the main actor and actress in your own play. What kind of plot will you create from this moment on with your partner?

BONUS SECTION

Want to Better Understand Your Spouse?

Try these revealing questions for date nights and couples' getaways.

Date nights and couples' getaways don't have to be expensive. Use the following questions to craft intriguing date nights or weekend getaways to grow your intimate connection.

Simply find a cozy spot for just the two of you to chat, take a walk holding hands, or enjoy coffee and something caloric. The important thing is, don't rush. Take your time answering these questions. They'll stir up scintillating discussions and prompt some aha moments between the two of you.

Your relationship will emerge stronger. You'll understand each other and the backgrounds that shaped each of you much more. Your empathy and sympathy will grow. You might even be overwhelmed with such gratefulness and love for each other that you fall into each other's arms and . . . (I'll leave the rest up to your creativity and imagination).

1. *How would you describe your parent(s)? For example:*

Mom: good at being in charge, always worked, yelled sometimes
Dad: liked things peaceful, loved books, rarely talked, kind of a
   pushover

Based on those descriptions, which personality type(s) is your mom? Which personality type(s) is your dad?

What strengths did each have? What weaknesses did each have? How can you see those strengths and weaknesses reflected in their interactions—positive and/or negative—with each other?

How did seeing those reactions and responses make you feel? Did they shape your view of marriage? If so, how?

2. *List in order all the children in your family of origin (including step-siblings, if any) with their ages. Add their personality traits, including your own. For example:*

Husband's Family

Will (husband), 35: likes things to be perfect, reliable, accountant

Nigel (brother), 33: easygoing, artist

Ben (brother), 32: charming, friendly, salesman

Barb (sister), 29: manipulative, demanding, a brat, to be honest

Wife's Family

Megan (sister), 39: bookkeeper, temperamental

Samantha (sister), 37: independent, competitive, career oriented

Joy (wife), 33: easygoing, depends on others, everyone likes me

How do each of your siblings reflect their birth order?

How has your birth order and the personality of your siblings affected your personality traits now?

3. *What were you like as a child, especially before you started first grade (if you can remember)? Is this similar or different to what you're like now? If different, what sparked that change? A family move, a divorce, some other trauma? Explain.*

4. *Think back to your childhood. What are the five most significant experiences or events you can remember? Share those memories with your partner.*

Got your answers? (And no peeking beforehand.)

Review your answers to Question 1.

Consider this information: The parent who had the most influence on you as a child is most likely the parent you described first. That's not to say you got along best with that parent. In fact, that parent may have been absent from home for most of your growing-up years but was still the most influential in your life, even if their influence was due to their absence and lack of involvement.

If in describing your parents you use superlatives or descriptions preceded by *very*—such as very smart or very pretty—this is often an indication that you value that trait in your own life.

Review your answers to Question 2.

Consider this information: Look for patterns or roles that are assumed by each of the children in your growing-up families. Now diagram your current family (yourself, your spouse, and any children). How does each person resemble one of your siblings— or you?

What first attracted you to your partner? Why do you think that is, based on your birth order and personality?

What needs do you fulfill for each other?

What personality traits cause friction? Why?

Review your answers to Question 3.

Consider this information: There are probably still aspects of the little boy or girl you once were in you. If you had to complete the statement, "I only count when . . . ," what would you say, and why?

If you had to complete that statement for your spouse, based on what they said about their childhood personality, what do you think they would say, and why?

Review your answers to Question 4.

Consider this information: Your earliest memories—that is, the farthest you can go back in time—are symbolic of the way you look at life.

If your first memory is negative, you'll tend to see things in a negative or pessimistic way. If *all* of your recollections are negative, it's fairly safe to assume that you have a negative outlook on life.

If all of your recollections are situations where you were the center of attention—people bringing you presents at Christmas, a birthday surprise, etc.—it's safe to assume that your lifestyle is centered on attention getting.

If some of your early recollections are of you breaking rules and regulations and being punished for those infractions, a good guess is that you're a controller. You've now learned to be good at keeping rules, and that's why you're not very flexible.

This is a fun way to play a Sherlock Holmes detective game with your spouse. You'll be amazed at how many surprising and true deductions you'll make, just by looking at the pattern of early memories.[1]

SECRET #10

Feelings Pull You Together; Judgments Push You Apart

The five things you need to know about feelings, getting behind your spouse's eyes, and how to be good and angry.

All of us have feelings. Sometimes we get those trampled on, and sometimes we trample on others' feelings. If you say you haven't ever done that, I'd love to meet you. You're a greater saint than Mother Teresa.

Feelings can be dicey and cause problems, so most of us have learned not to share them, or at least to share them very carefully. That's because, at one time, we revealed how we felt about an important issue, and someone pounced on us.

But we didn't start out that way. Kids are painfully honest about how they feel. Too honest, in many instances.

Like the time my son, Kevin, was two years old, and we had a couple over for dinner. As we were beginning to enjoy the meal, Kevy turned to Sande and asked, "Mommy, what's her name?"

Sande turned adoring eyes on our son. "That's Mrs. McVay."

"Oh," he said. "I hate her."

Yup, the dinner conversation stopped for a moment. Sande, the picture of social propriety, was nonplussed. It even stopped me for a moment as I lifted the fork to my mouth.

When we got to the bottom of that "feeling," we discovered that apparently *hate* was a new word he'd learned that day, and he was certainly open and free to share that feeling.

I'm not saying any of us should be *that* open in a relationship with all that's going on internally. However, most of us have gone too far in the other direction. We can't tell anyone how we feel without checking first to see which direction the wind is blowing.

Neil and Cary, a middleborn couple, are a good example of that. They've been married for five years, but there's not much intimacy happening in conversation or in anything else. It wasn't hard to figure out why when they told me what typically happened between them as they started snuggling. They'd each admit they were "kinda interested," but neither was quite sure how the other felt.

Here's the well-worn scene.

He reaches over and gives her a love pat. "Well . . . uh . . . good night. Love you."

"Love you too, honey."

They lie there for a moment.

Slowly she reaches over and pats him. "You feeling okay?"

"Oh, yeah, sure. You?"

"Fine."

Another couple moments of silence, then he asks, "Are you, uh . . . you . . . interested . . . ?"

"Well . . . yeah, sure . . . I guess."

"Unless you're too tired," he says.

"Oh, I'm not *that* tired. But if *you* are, it's okay, because I'm *kind* of tired . . ."

And they go on like that for a while until they finally fall asleep, exhausted from all the dancing around the subject.

Was this an exaggeration? Nope. That's exactly what happened between the two of them almost on a weekly basis.

The same type of thing happens in relationships across America every night. The husband can't bring himself to express his feelings to his wife, to say, "I love you, and I want to make love to you." The wife won't tell her husband that what she wants right now, more than anything else, is for him to hold her in his arms. And she wants him to talk to her on a daily basis about things that matter.

Communicating with each other and doing acts of love are critical to healthy, lasting relationships.

So both go on without what they really want and need, and that lack of communication leads to a blah, less-than, or battlefield relationship. Communicating with each other and doing acts of love are critical to healthy, lasting relationships.

Understanding feelings and how they work and don't work are also significant pieces in the puzzle of relationships and growing in your intimacy. In this chapter, we'll explore five secrets you need to know about feelings and how they affect you and your spouse.

#1: Feelings Aren't Right or Wrong

Feelings aren't right or wrong. They're just feelings. They aren't something you think about and process with your intellect.

When someone has hurt you, have you ever said to yourself, "Well, she said something bad about me, so I think I'm going to feel hurt for a while"?

No? Well, neither have I, and neither has anyone else on the planet.

If someone says something bad about you, you're automatically going to be hurt. That's just the way it is. A feeling is an emotional reaction that exists within you, whether you want it to exist or

171

not, whether you like the feeling or not. Having negative feelings doesn't make you a bad person, just as having positive feelings doesn't make you a good person.

Sometimes that natural inclination to show feelings is beaten out of us early in life. We're taught not to be rude, not to hurt others, not to get too excited, not to express too much affection, not to grieve, not to cry. As we mature, we may choose instead to intellectualize and rationalize why we can't or don't share our feelings. It's easier to be a plastic person than a real one. Since we're not used to sharing our emotions or seeing others share theirs, there's a distinct danger that we might be misunderstood.

> *Having negative feelings doesn't make you a bad person, just as having positive feelings doesn't make you a good person.*

Here's what I mean. If I walk up to a woman and say, "I think you're very beautiful," what's her immediate reaction? She might think one of these:

- *Well, I don't feel beautiful. I feel ugly, especially today.*
- *I wonder what this guy's up to. Why is he talking to me now, of all times?*
- *This guy's trying to manipulate me. All guys do.*
- *He must want something from me.*

Those are just a few immediate reactions I might trigger by my words. They were intended as an honest compliment, but they weren't received that way because of the woman's own background, personality, needs, mantra, and lifestyle.

Now, if I'm afraid that making such a comment would trigger any of these negative reactions in the person I approach, I might rationalize, "I'd better not express how I feel about her or I might cause some problems between us."

When the person you're interacting with in that way is your partner, you will never be able to grow an intimate connection.

172

Repress your feelings and one or both of you will pay for it—both physically and relationally. You'll get headaches, backaches, back spasms, muscle spasms, gastrointestinal disorders . . . and much more.

You can't help how you feel, and you have no reason to apologize for it. If you have negative feelings toward your partner and act them out in a hostile or harmful way instead of expressing them with loving, gentle communication, then you need to be held accountable for your actions. But there's nothing wrong with feelings in and of themselves.

#2: You Have a Right to Express Your Feelings

Since emotions are neither right nor wrong, you have a right to express them. The problem comes when no one wants to listen or you meet a great wall of resistance on the other end.

Jia, 24, knew all about that. Anytime she tried to even bring up her feelings of neglect, worry, frustration, fear, and anger to her partner, he'd tromp right over her attempt. In no uncertain terms, Joe would bluntly tell her, "Get off my case."

So I suggested to Jia that she try something creative and old-fashioned. It's called a handwritten letter, and few of them exist in our day and age. Since Joe wouldn't listen to her at home, she wrote a letter with her basic concerns, then FedExed it next-day to her husband's office.

The strategy worked. He was so shocked to get such a package that he tore it open and read the letter. All of it, in fact.

That night Joe walked in the door with a very different demeanor. He said softly, "I understand. And I'm sorry."

Jia's creative effort began the process of enabling this young couple to start a real conversation—one that can only happen when two people are contributing to it. So if you can't express yourself verbally, or if your partner won't listen to you, then why not try Jia's way?

One word of caution, though. Starting off with something like "Dear Nitwit" probably isn't the best option. I doubt that letter would be read. However, if you say what you need to say in as gentle and palatable a way as possible, you do your part to open a door to better communication instead of slamming it shut.

If you say what you need to say in as gentle and palatable a way as possible, you do your part to open a door to better communication instead of slamming it shut.

If your partner is opening up about his innermost feelings, try your hardest to be sensitive. You may not like what you hear, but it's important that you hear it. Many of us struggle with discomfort when we're forced to deal with true human emotion.

What do you do and say when a friend loses a loved one, for example? Do you brush her off with statements like:

- "I guess those things happen."
- "Must have been for a reason."
- "Now it's time to move on."

If so, you aren't very comfortable with the expression of feelings—whether your own or anyone else's. How much better would it be to simply say, "I'm sorry, and I care," to put your arm around your friend, or even to cry with her?

How do you begin to share your own feelings with your partner? And to open yourself up enough to hear and learn to understand how they feel?

First, be *willing* to do so. Make it a priority to take time to sit and talk with your spouse. Second, realize you can't read their mind, as much as you might think you know them. Third, realize that there are times when you have to tell and times when you have to ask. You can't develop an intimate connection without both of those happening.

Begin today to share your feelings with your spouse—in gentleness and love.

#3: You Don't Always Have to Act on Your Feelings

What do you do when someone cuts you off in traffic? Or your neighbor's dog leaves a present right in front of your apartment door again?

Maybe I don't want to know.

Just imagine what would happen if we all acted on impulse. One small act of violence would lead to another and another and so on, in an escalating spiral that would be more than messy. It would be horrific.

Although we all have the capacity to experience a full range of feelings, it's important to remember that we can choose *not* to act on them. Our world is tumultuous and terrible enough without all of us going around acting on every feeling we have.

> *Just imagine what would happen if we all acted on impulse.*

When we do act on our feelings, we're often doing it for a purpose—because we've gotten our way before through being powerful or explosive, or by choosing to withdraw or be moody.

Perhaps your depressed-acting partner complains all the time about not getting enough attention. But what she's really doing is exercising a neurotic type of attention getting. That's her way of keeping you on your toes and under her control.

I once had a guy in my office who admitted he acted unwisely. But then he defended his actions by saying, "Well, that's just the way I am, and there's not much I can do about it."

Wrong.

What he was really saying was, "I refuse to change. I'm not even going to try." How unfortunate for him and for his loved one.

You may feel angry, as though you want to punch someone in the nose. It's okay to feel that way. But what's not okay is acting on punching that person in the nose. It's important to find a way to express that feeling in an acceptable manner.

Suppose a service attendant in a restaurant is extremely rude to you. Annoyed, you consider reporting her behavior to the manager.

You also decide not to leave a tip, or to leave a very small one. But you're not handling the situation well if you trip her the next time she passes with a tray of food, or if you take a poke at her as you're on your way out of the restaurant.

How are you handling your annoyances with your partner? Do you handle your feelings well or in an underhanded or aggressive way? Finding an acceptable, constructive, nonthreatening, loving way to express your feelings to each other is critical to keeping any relationship healthy and growing. Here's some really great advice that's been around for many generations: "Don't let the sun go down with you still angry—get over it quickly."[1]

The next time you're driving on the expressway and someone cuts you off, you'll still be tempted. Those fiery feelings will rise to the surface. But what you do with them next is what will determine your life path—and that person's. So rise above your feelings. Decide not to engage in what could grow bigger.

Choose to do the right thing . . . with your spouse too. If you do, you'll avoid a lot of accidents and the subsequent fallout.

#4: Never Ask, "Why Do You Feel That Way?"

Why should you never ask, "Why do you feel that way?" Because it effectively ends a conversation. It sets up a defensive frown, narrowed eyes, crossed arms, a clamped mouth—all sorts of body language that show defensiveness and resistance, not to mention closed ears.

If you really want to know how your partner feels, you have to be willing to spend some time in honest dialogue. Asking why intrudes into your partner's thoughts and feelings and prevents you from going deeper. Asking why introduces a threatening edge into what otherwise could be an accepting environment. It puts the asker in a position of judgment over the other—at least, that's how it feels to the one being questioned.

In order to judge someone you have to be in a superior position, with the other in an inferior position. But relationships only work long-term and stay healthy if both individuals are equals.

What happened between Marcy and John is a good example of that principle. Every day when John returned from work, he said a lot of wonderful things about his secretary, Bonnie. Marcy tried her best to listen with good humor and accept that he was simply sharing something about his day.

Finally, though, she couldn't take hearing about another woman in such glowing terms anymore, especially when he never complimented her. Plucking up her courage, she decided to tell him how she felt.

John listened to about three sentences, then blurted out, "Why do you feel that way?"

Marcy ran from the room in tears.

That was the end of the conversation,

Why should you never ask, "Why do you feel that way?" Because it effectively ends a conversation.

but not the end of the problem. By asking why, John was bluntly telling his wife, "Your reaction is totally uncalled-for. It's completely incomprehensible to me . . . and more than stupid."

Even if he thought Marcy's jealousy was unfounded, he should have said something along the lines of, "I'm sorry you feel that way. I don't mean to hurt your feelings. Let's talk about it." He needed to spend time reinforcing the fact that his deepest love and respect were reserved for her and her alone, not for his secretary. Instead he had become defensive and basically pooh-poohed his wife's feelings. If he had known his wife as well as he should, he wouldn't have had to ask, "Why do you feel that way?" He'd already know it was because:

- He'd said too many good things about his secretary.
- Marcy loved him and feared another woman might be coming between them.
- She needed reassurance that she had the top spot in his life.

As for Marcy, she didn't stop to think, *I'm going to be jealous.* She just was. As we said earlier, feelings don't stem from the intellect (the mind); they come from the heart.

You don't have to always agree with everything your partner says. If you did, your relationship really would get stale and boring. However, out of respect and love, you should listen to each other, value each other's opinions, and seek to work out a solution to any problems.

Why should you not ask why? Simply stated:

- It inhibits communication.
- It implies the need to defend our feelings.
- It inhibits acceptance.
- It triggers defensiveness.

Those are certainly powerful reasons to tuck that *why* away when you talk with your partner.

#5: Getting Angry, Blaming Your Spouse, or Passing the Buck Doesn't Resolve Anything

The next time you have to wait in a long line, take a good look around you. See how the other people in the line are reacting.

Some will obviously be angry and muttering to others around them, "This is ridiculous! I can't believe we have to wait in this line." Others will be calm, collected, even serene. To those folks, it's an inconvenience to wait, but it's not the end of the world.

If you listen to what's being said, you're likely to find that the angry ones are blaming someone else for the problem:

"They have no right to make us wait like this."

"They should be better organized."

"Who do they think they are?"

Those who aren't angry aren't assessing blame. They're just thinking, *Well, these things happen sometimes, so I might as well make the best of the situation.*

Is it wrong to get angry, then? No, we all do at times, and our anger may be justified. But we also need to understand where our emotions come from and quit assessing blame for them.

"You make me so mad!"

"You drive me crazy."

"You made me do it."

Those statements are examples of how we sometimes pass the buck of blame on to our partner as the source of our anger or any other emotions. But the truth is, feelings are made, manufactured, and distributed by our own selves. Anger, joy, happiness, fear—every emotion comes from inside us.

Feelings are made, manufactured, and distributed by our own selves. Anger, joy, happiness, fear—every emotion comes from inside us.

Unfortunately, too many people are what I call "bone diggers." Long after the specific event is over and all the dust has settled in the backyard, if the bone digger isn't satisfied—if the true emotions and feelings are never expressed—they will take a shovel, go out to the backyard, and dig up the bones of those supposedly long-gone emotions.

Such an exercise is rarely productive, and it's usually divisive. If your marital relationship isn't based on openness, honesty, and forgiveness when hurt happens, then chances are good that it will continue to have adolescent-like tendencies. You'll deal with things like jealousy, accusations, bickering back and forth, angry explosions, and leaving in a huff.

One of the reasons we have trouble understanding our partner's feelings is that we layer those feelings with judgments, opinions, and values. Anytime we use "you" or "they" statements, we're passing the buck.

The next time you need to express your anger or frustration, use "I" statements rather than "you" or "they" statements: "I feel very angry when you say things like that." When you do that, you focus on your response and your feelings rather than the other person's actions. You might want to soften the sharing of your feelings even more by saying, "I'm not sure why I feel this way, but I'm feeling hurt" (or angry or left out—whatever you're feeling).

The next time you need to express your anger or frustration, use "I" statements rather than "you" or "they" statements.

Again, a healthy marriage is based on two equal partners—not a superior and an inferior. When you remove "you" and "they" statements, you remove judgment from the marital equation.

Think how fulfilling it would be if you could tell your partner any frustrations, concerns, and fears and know that they wouldn't judge you in any way for it.

How to Be Good and Angry

I exited the doors of a Walmart recently, right behind a woman pushing a shopping cart full of purchases and a boy walking beside her who looked like he was seven or eight years old. He was getting harangued.

"I don't know why you do such stupid things," his mother told him. "You make me so angry. I just hate to take you anywhere."

I had no idea what the boy had done, because I hadn't seen him do anything wrong. But his mother was clearly terribly angry and letting him have it.

The boy didn't say anything. He simply trudged along, but the slump in his shoulders said that he heard every word. He was already defeated, but still Mom wasn't through.

"I don't know why you have to mess up everything. You're just a . . . disgrace."

The woman's tirade continued as they reached their car, and she began to unload her shopping cart into the back seat. By now they were so far away from me that I could no longer hear what she was saying, but I could still detect the sharp, angry tone.

You know the ancient saying, "Sticks and stones may break my bones, but names will never hurt me"? Well, that's wrong. I'm quite sure every single one of her angry words was hitting that boy with the same force as a good-sized stone. Still, he didn't raise a whimper in protest. He simply soaked it all in as if he deserved every bit of it.

I sat in my car, debating briefly about whether to go over and talk to the woman. I don't usually like to butt into other people's affairs unless I'm asked, but I was beginning to think this might be a good time to make an exception.

By the time I processed that, though, the woman and boy were in their car and pulling out of the parking lot. I had hesitated a moment too long.

As I watched them drive by, I breathed a quick prayer to Almighty God that the woman would quit reacting to her child in this way, and that the boy would know he didn't deserve that kind of treatment.

Did the woman have a right to be angry? Maybe. As I said, I have no idea what the boy did. Still, let's assume he did something absolutely terrible, such as overturning a big display in the middle of the store on purpose after throwing a massive temper tantrum. Then perhaps his mother did have every right in the world to be angry with him.

But what was wrong with the situation was that the mother had no idea how to handle or control her anger. She was letting it pour out of her in ways that were destructive to the boy and to her role as his parent. What's more, she was focusing her anger directly onto the *boy himself* instead of on his *actions*, which she didn't appreciate and had evidently caused her so much trouble. Essentially, she was telling him that *he* was a disgrace, that she

IF YOU ARE BEING ABUSED

If your spouse is rough or abusive in any way, they don't deserve your respect. You absolutely should not put up with such behavior. You were not created to be a doormat for anyone to wipe their shoes on. That type of behavior in your home must stop—now. Leave immediately and go to a place where you and your kids will not be in danger. Let a professional help you sort things out. Your spouse needs a wake-up call to prompt a change in behavior. Before you can interact safely again—if that's even possible—you need to see a long track record of that changed behavior and a lot of rebuilt trust.

hated to go anywhere with him, and that he was stupid. She hadn't learned the importance of focusing anger on the *act* rather than the person committing the act.

We all get angry, and sometimes we have the right to be angry because of something our spouse has done. But having the right to be angry is not the same as having the right to lash out in retaliation at those who have angered you or to hurt them.

You have a right to express your anger . . . as long as you express it in ways that aren't destructive and will ultimately strengthen rather than destroy the other person and your relationship with them.

If you get angry with your partner, tell her she's stupid, and say she's always messing things up, you're out of line. If you say, on the other hand, "I really get angry when such and such happens," then you've helped to defuse the situation. You haven't said, "It's your fault," but rather, "I get angry . . ." That's a much better starting place for good communication than pointing a finger at your spouse.

Is your anger justified? Perhaps it is, and if so, then the other person needs to apologize and resolve to never again do what caused you to be angry.

Or perhaps you were so angry that you misunderstood the situation. If so, a careful explanation of the situation on both sides should alleviate any anger you're feeling.

A third possibility also exists: There's really no justification for your anger at all, and you're simply being unreasonable. You're human. It happens . . . to me too. If that's the case, when you come to your senses later, you'll feel a lot better if you haven't embarrassed yourself and hurt your spouse by stomping around, blathering about some situation that doesn't make sense, and accusing them of something that isn't true.

The key in expressing any anger is to point it toward the act, not the individual. It works with kids, and it also works with spouses to ratchet down the heated temperature in the house.

Many of us have never really dealt with anger. We've been taught to turn it inward, toward ourselves, keeping our real feelings inside. Then, in pressure-cooker fashion, the hurts, feelings, and frustrations begin to boil to the surface. We blow up, and our anger becomes destructive because it lashes out at anyone unfortunate enough to be in the way. Too often, the recipients of that anger are the ones we love the most—our family. It's important to get on the front end of anger management before we let our feelings blow over our partner or kids.

> *You have a right to express your anger . . . as long as you express it in ways that aren't destructive and will ultimately strengthen rather than destroy the other person and your relationship with them.*

If we can get to the point where we begin to share anger and frustration in a positive way, using "I" instead of "you" and "they" terminology, then our anger doesn't pass on to our spouse.

So how does this work?

Scenario #1

You arrive home, and you're in a bad mood. Your boss has been on your back all day. You walk in the door grumbling like a grizzly bear that was rudely awakened right in the middle of his winter nap.

Your spouse notices this right away and says, "Boy, are you ever in a bad mood!"

What would you usually say? "I am not!"

What does that accomplish? You're even more grouchy and angry because you resent the fact that you've been accused of being in a bad mood, even though it's 100 percent accurate.

You've just picked a fight with your spouse merely because she happened to get in the pathway of your anger and got steamrolled as a result. Now both of you are stomping down the hallway in opposite directions. Later you hear her yelling at the kids, then the older kid yells at your dog. . . . See how it all works? Why start the cycle in the first place?

What would a better option be? To confess, "You're right. I really am in a bad mood tonight. I'm angry and exhausted. Let me tell you why." Then you proceed to tell your spouse about the situation at work.

In this way, she becomes someone who can listen to you, sympathize with you, and help you deal with your feelings.

That, ladies and gentlemen, is how you gain an intimate connection that will only grow stronger.

Scenario #2

It's late on a Saturday morning, and you've got a busy day with lots to do, including vacuuming the house. Your husband is still sound asleep. You putter around the house, gradually making more and more noise because you think he ought to be up too.

Suddenly you decide, *Enough with this business of being subtle.* You stomp into the bedroom, throw open the curtains to the bright sunlight, and announce, "You ought to be up! It's nearly ten o'clock! How long are you going to lie in that bed anyway?"

Needless to say, this isn't going to get your weekend off to a very good start.

But suppose you choose another approach. Seeing that husband of yours still in bed, you go back to the kitchen. You make him a cup of his favorite coffee, bring it to the bedside, and begin to rub his back softly.

Yes, you're still angry. You resent him lying there all cozily when you've got so much work to do. Those feelings exist. You acknowledge them as what they are. But at the back of your mind you also consider the most important question: *Do I love him?*

You realize, *Yes, I do, so sometimes that will mean putting my own needs—like getting some help cleaning the house—on the back burner for a bit while I meet the needs of my husband.*

Giving him that coffee and a little back rub is going to make this a great Saturday for both of you.

Building a Bridge

Granting forgiveness when a partner hurts you is difficult. But holding a grudge is far more difficult and harder on you (and your partner) in the long run. It will also drive you apart. Is that really what you want? Or do you desire to move on and love in a healthy way?

Without the act of forgiveness, you can't be free of the hurt or have the option to change your actions toward the other person. So if you are the one offended, forgiving the offender is your part in the reconciliation. You won't be able to and shouldn't forget the offense, but you can choose to view it through a different lens. Yes, the event happened, you both have learned from it, and you have decided to move on together.

However, the two of you won't truly be united unless the offender does three things:

- shows they are truly sorry through both words and actions
- does their best to make restitution wherever possible

- works hard to rebuild your trust and belief over time by proving through their actions their choice to do things differently

In short, forgiveness is not a onetime event but an ongoing process of rebuilding broken trust for as long as it takes, reconciling a relationship, and choosing a different path.

The relationship you had before, which allowed the hurt, can't continue as is. You must actively choose to move on from where you are but take a different path.

For more, see "What Forgiveness Is Not" on page 250.

Responding versus Reacting

Responding and *reacting* are both actions, but the thought process—or lack thereof—behind them is completely different.

When you *react*, you are unconsciously relying on your background, prior experiences, personality, and resulting mantra and lifestyle to choose your action for you. You're acting instinctively, without thinking through the ramifications of your next move. But as we've seen in this book, acting without thinking, *What have I done before? Did it work? What should I do differently next time?* can not only harm you but also cause all kinds of problems in your relationship.

When you *respond*, though, you're choosing to act upon what you know about the person, their needs, and the situation in order to bring about a positive result. That's a far better way, and the only way to grow an intimate connection.

So do yourself a favor. Take a good look at yourself and your background, understand why you say and do what you do, and learn the fine art of responding rather than reacting. If you do so, you'll become a relational master. You'll know how to use feelings to pull you toward your partner and how to steer clear of judgments, which push you apart.

As you understand more about your spouse—their background, birth order, personality, and prior experiences—and how those factors influence their thinking, words, feelings, and behaviors, your marriage will be renewed from the inside out . . . with stellar results.

The Importance of Trust

To have a successful marriage and an intimate connection, you have to trust each other. Trust is a basic foundation of any relationship. You need to trust your spouse enough to be able to share some of the inadequacies you feel, some of the fears you have, some of your priorities in life, and some of the experiences that have shaped who you are. You also need to be comfortable sharing your feelings with that person.

Part of trust is telling the person who you really are and being willing to share your most intimate thoughts and feelings. It's like handing your partner a jewelry box full of precious stones and saying, "Here are my feelings. I'm going to share them with you because I know you'll take care of them. You won't dump them in the dirt, step on them, or throw them in the trash. You'll treat them as special and important."

Trust is a basic foundation of any relationship.

Sharing your feelings with your loved one isn't a one-shot deal. It's a continual process of unraveling the mystery of each unique individual. Every day we change, perceive different things, and develop different attitudes and feelings about life. That means every day we must be willing to share and discuss those changes with our loved one.

So let me encourage you to take a risk. Begin today to share your feelings with your spouse. As you do, listen for words like "you" and "they" that might indicate you're blaming your spouse for your feelings. If and when that happens (because it will, until you have more of a track record in your head for managing those pesky "you" and "they" and "why" words), apologize immediately. Say you need a minute or two to collect your thoughts, retreat for that time, and then meet again with your spouse.

Communicating your emotions, and accepting your spouse's emotions without feeling threatened or being judgmental, isn't always easy. But if you begin to honestly share your feelings and accept and support your loved one's, the two of you will discover that your relationship has hit a new high. No, you won't be perfect, but you'll have a greater awareness of your love for each other. And you'll be moving much closer to that intimate connection you're longing for.

The Choice Is Yours

Each of us has only so much energy to expend every day, and we have to decide exactly how we're going to use it. In love or in anger? Doing *for* others or doing *to* others?

Everything is more effective and longer lasting when it's done in love rather than anger.

Some couples live as if they're out in the center of a big pool, treading water. They aren't making progress in any direction. They're paddling like mad, but they're just not moving. That's because they're afraid to move from the one "safe" position they think they have. But if they tread water long enough, they're going to get tired. They can't do that forever or they'll go under.

Don't settle for blah or less-than in your marriage. And don't settle for a battlefield, either. You and your spouse deserve so much more.

Today's a good day to start doing what needs to be done in your marriage. Maybe you've never learned to communicate your emotions. Now's the time to practice sharing with your partner. Set up a special time each day when the two of you can talk together about

188

what's on your minds. Even better, make it a really special time—take a bath together.

Everything is more effective and longer lasting when it's done in love rather than anger.

Yes, I mean that. The bathtub is probably the best environment in the house to discuss any feelings. After all, it's very difficult to get up, run to the next room, and close the door (especially if anyone else is in the house). This setting also removes all barriers between the two of you (and you know what I mean). Somehow it's a lot more difficult to stay upset with each other if you're both sitting there in a grand Adam-and-Eve-in-the-garden state.

You might call me crazy. But I'm living proof that the strategy works.

BONUS SECTION

How to Find a Professional Counselor

You may decide that you need one-on-one professional help beyond what this book can give. That may especially be true if you've experienced abuse of any kind (whether childhood abuse, abusive dating partners or rape, or abuse in your marriage). If so, I encourage you to find a therapist who wants to get rid of you as soon as possible.

Yes, you read that right. Find a professional who wants to help you deal with the issues you have, can give you guidance on how to grapple with them, and then gets rid of you quickly. If a therapist can't help you get a handle on your issues in no more than 10 sessions, you need to hightail it out of there. They might be more interested in buying a new boat than in getting you on the right road.

First, get three or four recommendations from people you trust. Second, before you visit the office, call and ask a few key questions, the least important one being, "How much do you charge?" You aren't looking for the best price for a cell phone plan. You're talking about someone who is going to enter your very private world—a world vital to your well-being and the state of your marriage. To make sure you've found the right person, here are some questions I suggest you ask if their website doesn't already answer them:

1. Do you see couples together, individually, or both? Do you ever see the entire family? If so, at what stages?
2. How many sessions should we expect? How many minutes are each session? What is the fee per session? Do I pay per session or up front for a grouping of sessions?
3. What types of insurance do you accept?

191

4. What academic degrees and training do you have? Are you certified by the State Board of Psychologist Examiners or other appropriate boards? What are your professional affiliations?

5. What counseling methods do you use? Can you give me a brief explanation of what they are and why you use them?

SECRET #11

Marriage Isn't a One-on-One Competition; It's a Team Sport

How to identify negative moves in six power games and turn them into positive plays.

Who's winning your marriage? If it's one or the other of you, you're both losing.

Marriage isn't a competition. It's a team sport. However, for many couples, that team sport resembles a WWE match where there are no rules, and the takedowns are swift and underhanded. For wrestling fans, watching the WWE matches are light and fun entertainment. But in marriage, underhanded moves are anything but entertaining, because the ones you love the most can also get hurt the most by you. You know their weak points and exactly where to hit or tackle them. And since you live with those people, they're readily accessible as psychological punching bags for your bad moods, even if they didn't create those moods.

Sometimes couples unwittingly—or on purpose—play power games designed to conquer each other. But when you take a look at what those games really are, they have everything to do with not meeting each other's needs.

Game #1: Who's Right?

"I think we should do X," he says.

"No, that's wrong," she shoots back. "We should do Y, because what we did last time didn't work."

"No, but that's because . . . ," he throws back at her.

And the bickering continues.

What did either of them gain? Nothing. Both had a need to be right, and neither wanted to give up.

Did you wince a bit at the familiarity of that scenario? If so, you're not alone. It happens between couples all the time, especially if both are firstborns and highly competitive.

Other triggers come from previous damaging interactions with parents or others you care about. When they talked to you in a condescending way and insisted they were right, you didn't have any choice but to take it at that time. But now, when your spouse tries the same thing or gets on his high horse, trying to prove he's right, what happens? You instinctively rear back and go into full fight mode. You didn't like being taken advantage of back then, and you certainly don't want to put up with it now.

When somebody wins, you both lose.

But is the drive to be right, just to be top dog for a moment, worth hurting your spouse? When somebody wins, you both lose.

There's a swift way to end the Who's Right? game. Simply stop playing. Just say calmly, "Well, you could be right."

Your partner's jaw will drop. The room will go silent.

Playing table tennis isn't any fun without a partner to return the lobbed ball, is it?

Game #2: Turtle Shell Mamba

You can bottle hurt, disappointment, and trauma for a long time by sticking your neck back inside your hard shell and hiding. For some people, withdrawing is a natural response to hurt, just as fighting is a natural response for others. Eventually, though, those bottled emotions will come out.

Often the messy explosion hits a person who isn't even responsible for the initial hurtful situation—your spouse. This is especially true in situations of childhood abuse. Memories of the events and the deep-seated feelings that resulted can cause a lack of trust and a sense of disconnection from your spouse. And they may not even know why you're withdrawing.

Bottle that stress long enough, and it has to seek an outlet somewhere in the body. Some people pay for it through backaches, ulcers, tense shoulders, or migraines. Others internally stack up their hurts deep inside, trying to ignore the reality of their presence. They avoid any conversation about their background or issues that concern them because they fear confrontation or that the discussion won't go well.

Think about this for a minute: Do *you* like confrontation? Does anyone you know thrive on confrontation? I doubt it.

No one likes to be uncomfortable, and we certainly don't like people who make us feel uncomfortable. In fact, we try to stay far away from them physically and emotionally. Comfortability is an important part of being a couple. It's like wearing a favorite pair of slippers or your well-worn jammies. They make you go "ahh" since they're so familiar. You can relax.

> *Comfortability is an important part of being a couple. It's like wearing a favorite pair of slippers or your well-worn jammies.*

Take away comfortability, though, and it's like being a guest perched on an antique chair in your own home. You're afraid to make a move for fear of breaking something, and you certainly can't relax.

That's why moving away from the Turtle Shell Mamba is so difficult. Stick your neck out of that shell and you're very vulnerable. What if you try to explain how you feel and what you think and get shut down? If you stay inside that shell, you're safer. Your life mantra has become, "The best way to not get hurt is to not even participate."

Perhaps you tried reaching out to others in childhood or in a past relationship and it didn't go well. Or you used to bring up ideas for improving your relationship and they were dismissed. Now you'd just rather stay comfy and protected inside that shell.

But let me ask you a simple question: Do you consider yourself worth loving? Do you really? If so, it's time to ask yourself some tough questions. Is your lack of communication with your spouse because you don't trust them? If so, why does that lack of trust exist? From your childhood experiences? From negative events with an ex-spouse or ex-boyfriend or ex-girlfriend? If there's no trust between two people, there can be no growing, lasting relationship.

Perhaps you took a lot of psychological and emotional notes while watching how your parents interacted as you were growing up. Or you endured a succession of a parent's live-ins who didn't treat you all that well. Perhaps your ex majorly did you wrong.

If there's no trust between two people, there can be no growing, lasting relationship.

Those are all unsettling experiences that have cemented into you the perspective that nothing is lasting or permanent. Since that's the case, you reason, you'd better keep your guard up and not allow anyone else close to you. If you do and they leave, it'll hurt too much.

Many of those experiences that have significantly impacted you started in childhood. Think of it this way. Buy a plant at a nursery, and the expert there will give you advice on how to nurture it—how much to water it, what kind of soil to plant it in, how much

A GOOD DEFINITION OF **INSANITY**

Insanity: doing what doesn't work over and over again.

Why, then, do we play out the same relational games in marriage if there's no track record of success? It's time to try something new.

plant food it needs. But do all kids get that much care in their home when they're growing up?

Many of you have grown up in homes that resemble a different type of planting experience. It's as if your parents picked up a plant from a discount store and halfheartedly dug a hole in the ground. That hole wasn't deep enough or wide enough for all your little plant roots, but oh well, at least it was a hole. Then they placed you in that hole and haphazardly tossed a little dirt over your roots. When they happened to think of it, they dribbled a bit of water on you. Six months later, you looked a little shriveled, but they didn't always notice.

Any plant or child can initially look good, but neither will stay looking good unless you take care of it. The same is true of marriages.

If you didn't have the kind of nurturing you craved during childhood, there's no one better to help you than the spouse who loves you and is in the trenches with you. Risk telling them about what happened to you. Say that you struggle with trust and betrayal and that you worry about permanency. Talk together about what each of you can do to increase your trust and intimacy.

For you, a big step will be risking trying new things and opening up in communication. For your spouse, a big step will include patience and not being hurt if you are slow to respond or reticent to try any suggestions.

If you're longing for an intimate connection, it's time to take a risk. I'd like to invite you to take even a tiny step out of that turtle shell. All it takes is a few words to your partner: "I'd like your help on something. . . ."

Game #3: Dump Truck

This game is just like the name sounds, and it's as childish and dirty as two kids slinging mud pies at each other.

Each spouse has a dump truck full of all kinds of stinky, rotten garbage heaped up as ammunition against the other. The philosophy is simple: "If you aim your dump truck in my direction, then you can bet I'll aim mine in your direction. What's more, I'll make sure the pile dumped on your head is even bigger."

That, folks, is human nature at its finest. Such behavior happens every day in marriages across the country. Problem is, it's a game of tit for tat, which can rapidly escalate into an all-out war.

Kate and Ron are a good example. I always knew when this couple was heading to my office, because I'd hear four-letter words ricocheting down the hallway. The couple had only been married three and a half years, but each of them had developed huge loads in their dump trucks.

They both were powerful, but in vastly different ways. Kate had an explosive temper. On more than one occasion she'd punched her fist through the plasterboard walls of their home. When she ramped up, all Ron could do was try to stay out of her way until she calmed down. In the meantime, he'd agree to anything she wanted. He'd received so many verbal onslaughts that he was almost immune to them. Anyone watching him being caught in the force of her wind would have felt tremendously empathetic toward him.

But Ron had his own dump truck. Though he was as passive in personality as she was aggressive, he'd heaped a lot of garbage up for ammunition too. After all, power doesn't come only in loud packages. It's also disguised by quiet, manipulative control. That was Ron. He was proud of the fact that he had a master's degree while his wife had only finished a year of community college. He had a habit of using his large vocabulary and knowledge of bigger issues to make her feel dumb and insignificant.

Her response to those continual put-downs? She'd adopted a private logic that went something like this: "If you have the right to put me down, then I have the right to put you down."

Ron's shrugs spoke volumes about his real thoughts and feelings.

Back and forth the two would go. It was sort of like playing poker. Someone places a bet and another chimes in, "I'll see your bet and raise you two."

The negative power plays between the two cycled over and over, like reruns from a bad movie on Groundhog Day.

You see, revenge is a two-edged sword. You may hurt someone else when you use it, but you're likely to hurt yourself in the process too. In any marriage relationship, revenge is a deadly tactic. Play that game long enough and you'll be buried under a garbage heap. The end result is not only losing affection for each other but not even caring one way or another about anything taking place in your relationship.

> *Revenge is a two-edged sword. You may hurt someone else when you use it, but you're likely to hurt yourself in the process too.*

The only way for this game to stop is by realizing what such fighting really is— an act of cooperation. Any game takes two. If you've gotten good at one-upping each other, then it's time to try cooperating in a new way . . . agreeing to stop the game.

Game #4: "You're Not the Boss of Me"

Kate was also a master at this game, and Ron was an expert at playing along. Because she felt inferior to Ron, she went out of her way to control him and show who *really* was boss in their marriage.

I saw Kate's anger firsthand, so I knew how scary it could be. But one event that occurred in my office was a game changer for both of them.

Occasionally in therapy, clients will get the idea that the psychologist is supporting the views of one spouse more than the other. Kate thought I was doing just that, and it wasn't in her favor. Her fury sparked. She called me a nasty name and left the office in a huff, slamming the door behind her. At least she controlled herself enough not to take a swing at me or punch her fist through one of *my* walls.

Right before she'd exited, she'd thrown a last definitive verbal punch: "I'll just walk home."

That was all of eight miles, and she was in no physical shape to do so. However, she wanted us to feel her wrath. She wanted us to know we'd made her feel uncomfortable and guilty. She wanted us to pay. In short, she wanted to be the boss of the situation.

Ron behaved as he usually did in such situations. He sprang out of his seat to go after her, calling, "Honey, you don't mean—"

I literally grabbed him by the seat of his pants. "Sit down," I ordered. "Is this typical? This is the kind of thing that goes on in your home?"

"All the time," he admitted. Kate was always throwing tantrums of one sort or another.

So I talked turkey with him. "If you really want things to turn around in your marriage, you need to begin behaving differently. There's no time like the present."

He swallowed hard and remained in his seat. I could tell that he was nervous about it, but he agreed with me that he'd let her attempt to walk home.

"If you really want things to turn around in your marriage, you need to begin behaving differently. There's no time like the present."

At the next visit I found out what had happened next.

Kate left the office like a steamroller. She'd been convinced that soon Ron would be not far behind in their car. He'd drive slowly beside her, saying how sorry he was and begging her to get in the car. It was a tried-and-true replay.

But that wasn't what happened. She walked and walked, with no sign of her husband. Meanwhile, I was keeping Ron hostage in my office.

Then, at an intersection about a mile from my office, something surprising happened. Kate fell into a construction hole. (Yes, this really is a true story.) She ended up breaking her leg in two places and lying there until sometime after 2:00 a.m., when someone finally heard her cry for help. That person called 9-1-1, and Kate was transported to the nearest hospital for emergency treatment.

Meanwhile, Ron was home. He had no idea where his wife was, but he was used to such behavior. She had frequently disappeared over their years of marriage—to punish him and make him feel guilty for anything he'd done. Once I explained to Ron how she was using such behaviors to manipulate him and stay in the driver's seat, he got the picture. But it was still hard for him not to constantly check his cell phone for messages or calls. Finally, he fell asleep, with no idea that his wife was in danger or in pain.

Just before dawn he was awakened with a phone call. Someone from their local hospital was calling, explaining that his wife had broken her leg and asking if he could come to the hospital.

Ron's immediate response was programmed: "I'll be right there." Then, as soon as he hung up, he hurriedly started to dress.

As he headed downstairs, though, he started thinking, *What would Dr. Leman suggest?* As hard as it was to go against his long-entrenched patterns, he decided to turn off his phone and get a few more hours of sleep.

It wasn't until 10:00, during regular visiting hours, that he finally sauntered into Kate's hospital room.

Her mood definitely hadn't improved by her lying in a hole for several hours with a broken leg. Her first words to her husband aren't printable. The next ones were, "When I get out of here, I'm going to break your neck!"

But she didn't. To this day, Kate says it was that particular incident that triggered her to begin making much-needed changes in how she related to her husband. Interestingly, Ron doing the unexpected—removing his sails from Kate's wind—was the action that precipitated the change.

Changes weren't easy for the two of them, but small steps led to larger steps. They stopped dumping on each other. Slowly they began to build a better relationship. A month later, they went shopping to buy a new set of dishes, since she'd broken most of theirs by throwing them at Ron.

Then came the day, several months later, when I saw the results of their hard work. The couple stepped hand in hand into my office. Kate was carrying a beautifully wrapped package, which she extended to me. It was a photo of the two of them, smiling, with their arms wrapped around each other.

"We want you to think of us when other couples come to you for help," Kate said.

"Yeah, if you can help hard cases like us, you can help anyone," Ron added. He winked at her, and she kissed him on the cheek.

The transformation was stunning. They had gone from an all-out war that even the best diplomat couldn't negotiate to the kind of intimate connection that cast a literal glow around them. No one who saw them now could have guessed where they'd been just a few short months earlier.

There's no time like the present to start your own marital transformation.

You can be at that place too. There's no time like the present to start your own marital transformation.

Game #5: Kill the Umpire

Have you ever been to a baseball game and seen a play nobody could quite figure out? One manager runs out of the dugout and argues that the play should be called his way. The other manager exits his dugout just as quickly and argues vehemently that the call should go in his favor.

Meanwhile, the umpire pulls the almighty rulebook out of his pocket and feverishly flips pages, trying to find the proper solution to handle the disagreement.

Of course, it doesn't matter what judgment that umpire makes. One of those managers will wind up being very angry and will be on the umpire's case for the rest of the game. Or at least until the ump gives him the old heave-ho and sends him to the locker room.

Some couples also play Kill the Umpire. When a man and woman get married, each brings their own rulebook. No, it's not in paper form; it's an internal little book with all the rules for life and marriage that each partner expects the couple to live by. Problem is, most couples don't share their rulebook with each other, because they're not even aware they have one. Yet each spouse has specific expectations of roles they should play and how things should go in their marriage.

Because couples haven't talked about the rules in their little books, they plunge into marriage in trial-and-error fashion. If one spouse violates an unwritten rule in the other's book, the one offended eventually becomes like that umpire, who will no longer put up with nonsense from a belligerent manager.

"One more move like that, and you're outta here!" A pointing finger accompanies the raised voice.

Why don't we talk about the things that matter most? Frankly, because talking about thoughts, feelings, and intimacy is . . . well . . . embarrassing. Especially if we were reared in homes where we were taught that showing physical affection should only be for the bedroom and for the act of sex.

Why don't we talk about the things that matter most?

Unless you know what's in your spouse's rulebook, you can never meet their needs. That, after all, is your greatest mission in marriage—to meet each other's needs in every way possible. You can only do that if you can communicate your expectations and needs and come to understand each other. In other words, you

203

need to open up those rulebooks to each other and reveal what's inside. If you don't transcend those rules and mythical limits, you'll never reach a mutually satisfying marriage.

Game #6: Take That, You Rat!

Ed, a successful businessman, called me one day to say he'd like to talk. "My partner and I have a few minor communication problems."

"Then let's talk," I said. "When can you both come in?"

He insisted that he wanted to come in first by himself.

"That's not the way I usually work," I told him but finally agreed to defer to his judgment.

When Ed and I met, he told me about his work, his travels, and all the activities he was involved in. I wondered how he found time to do all that, or even to eat a meal with Toni. He sounded simply too busy.

Yet when he spoke of Toni, his eyes glowed with pride. It was obvious he loved her very much. "She's beautiful, warmhearted, and capable at so many things," he explained. Then he paused. "But I guess she's also a bit . . . immature."

"What do you mean by 'immature'?" I asked.

"Well, she doesn't really understand all I do or how busy I am. Sometimes she gets upset." He went on to explain that there had been a number of petty issues lately that had mushroomed into full-grown squabbles. "I think we need to make some adjustments in our relationship, but I don't know what to do," he admitted.

Since he was still reticent for them both to come together, I made an appointment alone with Toni. The majority of the session was spent trying to get her to open up to me about her thoughts and feelings. She did tell me that she'd recently started a new job and really liked it. Then, as often happens, she dropped a bomb five minutes before the end of the session.

"I suppose if this is going to do any good, I need to be honest."

What poured out in a torrent wasn't surprising. Toni felt resentful and angry toward Ed, whom she declared was too busy to even care about her. "Truth is, a guy at work is looking really good to me."

I wasn't surprised. She'd received no attention from Ed for years, so even attention from a rock would look attractive.

"What do you like about the guy at work?" I asked, already knowing the likely answer.

She smiled. "Well, he takes the time to listen to me. He asks how my day is going. He even notices when I'm wearing something new and compliments me. He's gentle and kind. And he actually looks into my eyes."

It was an affair in the making if that man had even an ounce of interest in Toni. The very needs he was meeting for Toni were the ones Ed had neglected.

When we dug further into her background, we uncovered her life mantra: "I only count when I'm being noticed and when others are paying attention to me."

Toni was the baby of her family, used to being in the spotlight and catered to. Her family's world had revolved around her in the home she grew up in, and she felt she was now being ignored.

Ed was a firstborn, competing to win in every area of his life. He'd just forgotten that he needed to pay attention to Toni too.

If the man or woman you love isn't getting attention from you, it's an open door to get attention from someone else.

If the man or woman you love isn't getting attention from you, it's an open door to get attention from someone else. Even if your partner doesn't seek that attention, the temptation will be there, lurking in the shadows, because their needs are not being met. No one who's in a relationship just falls into the arms of another man or woman. They end up there because of a reason. Most of the time that reason is their partner's lack of attention to their core needs.

See why knowing your partner's needs is so important?

Anyone who walks with eyes open into an affair would be better advised to do something a bit safer, such as wrestling alligators in the swamps of Florida. Anyone who thinks, *No one will get hurt, and no one has to find out about it*, is living in a dream world and has never experienced real consequences for their actions.

As many of you who've already experienced affairs and the pain of losing a prior relationship know, no matter how an affair starts, it turns into a raging forest fire that destroys everything in its path. When an affair is revealed, trust breaks down because of the betrayal. Suddenly every act of your spouse is suspicious (and rightfully so). Even if a spouse doesn't find out, the partner who had the affair lives with a heavy burden of guilt, a broken heart, and divided loyalty. The couple is driven farther apart, often without one of them knowing why. Putting a relationship back together after such an event is far from easy, but it's possible—with time, a lot of patience, and a boatload of love.

Several years ago a man came to me for advice. He and his wife had been married for seven years, but he'd had an affair sometime back.

"When was that affair?" I asked.

"Four years ago," he said, a bit embarrassed.

"How long did it last?"

"Three months. Then I realized that not only was it wrong to do this, but it was destructive to the relationship I have with Ginger. I really love my wife, but . . ."

"You feel guilty?" I prompted.

He nodded. "Yeah."

"So play your own shrink. Why do you think you had an affair with that other woman?"

"I figured that out. It was because I was trying to meet a void in my life—something I needed that I wasn't getting from Ginger."

"And what was that need?" I pressed.

"Attention. Ginger goes through cycles where she's really busy at work, and to be honest, I feel ignored," he admitted. "So the other woman looked good to me . . . for a while."

So, reader, let me ask you, if Ginger doesn't already know about that affair four years ago, then what's the purpose of sharing it with her?

If she's like any person in a relationship, she'd want to know more details:

"How could you do such a thing?"

"When did it happen?"

"Who was it with?"

"How did it start?"

"Don't you love me anymore?"

"What exactly did you do with her?"

I'm not convinced that telling your partner about an affair that happened years ago is always the wisest option. Would you really want to know everything your partner did while dating someone else? Would it make you feel better to know? Would it draw the two of you closer . . . or push you apart?

Think of it this way. You have the flu. You tell yourself, "I'd feel better if I could just throw up." Finally you throw up, and you do feel better. Problem is, you aimed that vomit at the person you love, and now they're covered in it. Do you think they feel good about it?

In relationships, pouring out everything you did with another person, in detail—with how, when, why, and where—is like vomiting all over them. They have to live with the stench for a long time.

However, if your partner already knows about the affair, and you believe that it's possible for your relationship to withstand such betrayal and then move on from there, it's critical that the following steps take place.

First, if you had the affair, you need to accept responsibility for your actions and the breakdown of trust with your spouse. That means giving the person you love time to work through the resulting trauma in their own way and on their own timetable, without saying things like, "I told you it's over, and it's over. Why can't you believe me? You still don't trust me?"

I wouldn't trust you either, frankly. You'd have to prove your loyalty to me over and over before I could be drawn into your circle again.

Second, you need to end the affair. Period. That means telling the other person that you will be meeting them only one more time in a public place or making only one more phone call to state, "This is over. I'm sorry I've caused you hurt, but I know this is wrong. I cannot continue this affair. This is the last time we will meet or talk." And you walk away, delete that person's phone number and any other contact information, and don't look back.

Third, you go home immediately and say, "It's done." You draw your spouse into your arms and say, "I'm so sorry I caused you pain. I know it may be hard for you to believe this right now, but I love you. I will always love you. And I want to spend the rest of my life proving it to you."

You expect tears, angry words, and silences as your spouse processes their hurt, but you choose to move on from there. You eliminate anything that reminds you of your affair—gifts, photos, perfume, even visits to the coffee shop where you met. If you have to switch jobs to avoid seeing that person, then do so. It's a small price to pay for the pain you've caused your loved one, and it also will show them that you mean business.

Fourth, you spend every day being thankful for the man or woman you love, and that they're allowing you to remain as a partner in spite of your actions. Focus on meeting their needs. Be patient. Time does help to heal wounds. What matters most of all is that you change your trajectory. You need to do over and over what makes that person feel special, worthwhile, desirable, and uniquely needed in your universe.

Then you wait.

And wait again.

And keep doing more acts of love.

Because affairs are so damaging to trust in relationships, it's critical that partners avoid the slightest opportunity for an affair to even begin. Meaningful communication and acts of love are the two greatest deterrents to affairs.

Rick and Natasha have both traveled far and wide, independently, for their careers over the 20 years they've been married. But both have an ironclad agreement that neither will be alone in a hotel room with anyone of the opposite sex for any reason. Because of that trust, they can travel freely, get their work done swiftly, and never have to worry about what's going on with the other. They also make sure to touch base by phone every night, no matter where they are, to keep their hearts close. When they land back home, they make a point of taking a staycation, where they enjoy time off just with each other.

Meaningful communication and acts of love are the two greatest deterrents to affairs.

Evan and Mona are another stellar example of a couple who works hard at maintaining an intimate connection. Every weekday, during his 10:00 a.m. work break, Evan calls his wife to check in. They use the time to laugh together or empathize with each other about any antics of the morning and talk about upcoming plans for the evening. That way they stay on the same page daily even when they're apart. And it clears the deck to talk about even more meaningful things in the evening—dreams, future plans, etc.—instead of merely filling each other in on who needs to be where and when.

Here's the kicker. Evan has made that phone call for 32 years, 5 days a week.

Now that's dedication to your marriage.

Turning Negative Moves to Positive Power Plays

How can you curb any games you might be playing with each other?

- Start with a simple conversation, face-to-face. Truth is, some things in your marriage need to change.
- Get your rulebooks on the table, out in the open.
- Talk about your individual needs and expectations.
- One at a time, without the other interrupting, explain how you feel when your needs are not met. Inform gently; don't accuse.
- Develop your listening skills—listening to words, watching body language, reading each other's eyes.
- Commit together to use "we" language and thinking.
- Give up the need to be right or have the upper hand.
- Don't dig up the past after you've dealt with it.
- Communicate in an open, honest, and kind fashion— nothing hidden.
- Major on acts of love, large and small. Every day, say with your actions, "I love you."

Positive Games to Play to Your Heart's Content

- Write "You're mine forever" on the bathroom mirror in the steam or with lipstick. Draw a heart around it.
- Take a shower together.
- Hand-deliver your partner's favorite treats to their workplace.
- Give each other massages after a long day.
- Eat one bowl of ice cream with two spoons.
- Go away for the weekend—somewhere, anywhere. The goal? To be alone . . . together.

CREATE A **LOVE LIST**

There's nothing sweeter to a loved one than feeling like she's your number-one priority on your day off. Why not create your very own Love List—special things you can do for your spouse that uniquely suit her? Below is the list that Micah, a 37-year-old construction worker, came up with for his wife of 13 years.

Micah's Saturday Love List

- Serve her coffee—hazelnut, her favorite—in bed.
- Leave a new shower gel with a ribbon tied around it in the bathroom.
- Make Swedish pancakes from her mother's recipe.
- Clean and vacuum her minivan.
- Make tacos for lunch, since she's been craving Mexican food.
- Take her Rollerblading in the park. (She's been dying to go.)
- Share a strawberry-banana smoothie.
- Watch her favorite movie, complete with snacks from the fridge, freezer, and cupboards and served on our best plates.
- Finish the night with a back rub.

Shower gel: $7.99
Smoothie: $4.49
The rest: free!

Pretty creative for a couple who's on a tight budget, right? Kudos to that man. His wife's got to be one of the happiest women on the planet after that kind of day.

- Take a walk in the rain without an umbrella. (Those wet clothes will be dying to be removed.)
- One-up each other in writing a sweet note a day.
- Tell your spouse every day something you're thankful for about them.

- Choose a day to shower your partner with little surprises. They don't need to be expensive—just things you know will please your spouse.
- Make a Love Jar. Each spouse picks a different color of Post-its or paper. On those papers, write notes about things you'd like your partner to do with and for you. Every weekend, when you're sipping coffee or tea, take one slip of each color out of the jar. Make plans—that weekend, if possible—to do those activities. (You can have a lot of fun with this game. Take it from someone who knows!)

SECRET #12

For Your Spouse to Truly Hear You, You Have to Talk in a Way That Encourages Them to Listen

Why miscommunication happens, and how you can cure it before it causes trouble.

I recently saw a comic strip about a couple sitting in a marriage counselor's office. The counselor had given the couple a take-home assignment of communicating more during the week.

It hadn't gone so well.

The wife complained that the husband hadn't done what he was supposed to do. He'd said only three things to her all week: "Where's my dinner?" "Where's the remote control?" and "What's that smell?"

The husband shot back that the wife had said only two things to him: "You're sitting on it" and "Your socks."

The counselor looked at the husband and asked, "And which one of those answers had to do with 'Where's my dinner?'"

The exchange was funny for a cartoon, but it's not so funny in real life.

The typical married couple spends fewer than five minutes a day in real communication. Most conversations after work, even with the chattiest of couples, look a little like this:

The couple meets at the end of the day, when the latest one walks in the door from work.

Partner #1: "Hello! I'm home! How was your day?"

Partner #2: "Fine. How was yours?" (He knows she really isn't interested in hearing about the hassle he had with a coworker that day.)

Partner #1: "Okay." (Truth is, there were some really big problems at work, but she's spent the day having to hash over them with her colleagues, and she doesn't want to plow over the same ground right now.)

Partner #2: "What should we have for dinner?"

Partner #1: "I don't know. What do you want to have?"

Partner #2: "Should we do takeout, or do you want to go out to eat?"

Partner #1: "Let's just do takeout."

Partner #2: "Great."

Now, wasn't that a scintillating conversation? Basically, both have shown that they're not really interested in sharing the details of their lives with each other.

Four Reasons Couples Don't Communicate

Does any of the above exchange sound familiar? If so, you're not alone. The average couple majors in a lack of communication. But there are good reasons couples don't communicate.

Reason #1: They don't know how.

"Hey, I'm home!"

"Where's the mail?"

"What's for dessert?"

The partner who walks in the door and yells any of these things, especially in rapid-fire fashion, reveals something more than impatience. They show an appalling lack of communication skills.

Most of the time those words convey, "I'm just interested in you noticing I'm home and telling you what I need. But I don't really have any interest in getting feedback from you or carrying on a discussion."

Not knowing how to communicate is the most prevalent reason for the lack of communication between husbands and wives. Most of our conversations in life are superficial unless we've been schooled otherwise. If neither spouse grew up in a home where life issues were discussed in a loving, straightforward manner, then they haven't learned how to communicate with each other. Many couples simply don't know how to talk about anything other than what's for dinner or the weather.

> *Many couples simply don't know how to talk about anything other than what's for dinner or the weather. The good news is, we're trainable.*

The good news is, we're trainable.

Reason #2: They're afraid.

Many couples fear sharing their real selves with each other.

"If I tell him what I really think, he won't understand."

"If I tell her how I really feel, she'll reject me."

Rita, for example, was completely uninterested in politics and attending any sort of big wingdings, as she called them. But after she got married, her businessman husband became actively involved in politics and was asked to attend a lot of red-carpet events. Worse, he would surprise her with showy dresses that she considered too ostentatious to wear to the events. She was embarrassed that he was trying to show her off.

When he got a huge promotion, he surprised her again for her birthday—by buying her a red convertible sports car. She was a Honda Civic gal and liked the old version she'd had for nine years. The new car was simply too flashy for her tastes, but she was forced to drive it since he'd traded her Civic in without asking her.

Her anger and resentment came to a head with that vehicle purchase. But she didn't know how to tell her husband how much she hated the car and the dresses. All she'd wanted was a new coffeemaker since the one in their kitchen had developed a crack.

I encouraged her to talk to him. She was afraid she might back out if she didn't force herself into moving forward, so she told her husband ahead of time that she needed to talk to him about something. She chose a late-night dinner at a romantic restaurant.

When it was time for her to say what was on her mind, the words wouldn't come at first. But then, as she began to express her innermost feelings, the entire torrent rushed forth.

Her husband was stunned. After all, she'd done such a good job of acting for all these years that he thought she loved being in the spotlight, and he'd been trying to do nice things for her.

At first he was angry, defensive, and hurt. Why hadn't she told him this a long time ago?

Then Rita did what I'd told her to do. She reached out, took his hand, and told him how much she loved him. It was because she loved him and wanted to connect intimately with him that she had to tell him how she felt.

That affirmation of love calmed him and helped him begin to see her point of view. He said how proud he was of his beautiful wife and admitted that he liked to show her off. But his actions had only been meant to say, "Hey, everybody, this is my wonderful wife, and I love her." He even admitted he often felt unworthy of her and gave her all those fancy gifts as a means of making up for some lack he perceived in himself.

That discussion was the beginning of a whole new era of openness and honesty in their relationship. Changing their trajectory as a couple wasn't easy, though. He didn't want to give up all his political involvement, but he promised to cut back. She'd attend with him sometimes—and get to pick her own dress—but stay home other times. He'd be more attentive to her needs and desires.

Their growing love story continues to this day.

Every couple has rough spots to work through. All of us have weaknesses, fears, hurts, anger, and other things deep inside that we're embarrassed to reveal to others. But having those things doesn't make us bad or inferior. It simply makes us human.

REAL SELF VERSUS IDEAL SELF

There's always a difference between your "real self" (the person you really are) and your "ideal self" (the image you want others to see).

Draw a vertical line down the middle of a piece of paper. Write "Real Self" on one side and "Ideal Self" on the other side.

Take a few minutes to scribble down your thoughts. Who are you really? Put those adjectives and other descriptions under "Real Self."

Who do you want your spouse and others to think you really are? Write those adjectives and other descriptions under "Ideal Self."

Then ask yourself: What discrepancies do you see between your "real self" and your "ideal self"? How might those discrepancies cause tension in your marriage? Make some notes about your brainstorms.

If your spouse is also open to doing this exercise, then, after each of you has done the above steps individually, switch papers and read each other's. Discuss any descriptions that surprise you. Then talk about the ways the discrepancies you've discovered could cause misunderstandings or miscommunications between the two of you . . . and, if so, how you could resolve them before they happen.

After doing this exercise, you'll be amazed how much you learn about yourself and your spouse . . . and you'll lessen misunderstandings and improve your communication, too.

Reason #3: It's too much trouble.

If you try to share something about yourself, only to find out that the person listening doesn't really seem to care or shoots back a hurtful remark, what's naturally the first thing you think? *Well, I'll never share my feelings again.*

That kind of hurt happens in marriages every day. It may be pushed beneath the surface of a person's life, but it will never be buried so deeply that it won't cause some emotional and psychological problems.

Think of your emotional self as a teakettle on a stove, with the steam being your emotions and feelings. If you don't have the opportunity to let your emotions and feelings out in a constant, free-flowing manner, sooner or later you get to the point where you blow your top.

Lucy had been married multiple times. She was good at picking men who could best be described as losers. She'd divorced for the first time when she was 19, the second time at 23, and the third time at 28.

Her first husband was a shiftless, unfaithful, irresponsible man who left her when she got pregnant. Only four months after her divorce was final, she married Al. Then she found out he had a problem with drugs, which eventually cost him his job. He wasn't faithful either. Then she met Rowdy Raymond, who had all the charm of her first two husbands, as well as a violent streak.

When we evaluated her early life, including her parents, siblings, and memories, it was clear why Lucy was picking such men. She was reinforcing her life mantra: "I'm not worth loving." Her father had never shown her any affection, because that wasn't the way men were supposed to act. She had an older brother and older sister who were both seemingly perfect.

Lucy decided early on that there was no way to be the best, so she might as well be the worst. She found her niche by being truant from school, giving people a hard time, and basically giving her parents' strict moral values a good, strong kick in the teeth. Her flippant attitude said, "I don't give a rip about anything." But it wasn't that she didn't care. She cared deeply. She just didn't think anybody else would be interested in what she thought. If they knew the things on her mind, they might make fun of her, and that risk wasn't worth the trouble. So she hid her real thoughts and hurts behind a rough exterior.

When I told her she was purposefully selecting men who were no good for her, who would mistreat her and behave in an unloving manner toward her, she was skeptical. "Why would anyone marry someone they knew would mistreat them?"

I answered, "Well, people do that because they're following the rules of a lifestyle that says, 'I'm not worth anything,' 'I deserve to be abused,' and 'Nobody could possibly care about what *I* think!'"

That's when I saw the first chink in Lucy's armor. In subsequent sessions, she realized that the driving forces in her life were to get a man's attention, because she'd never had the attention of her father. It didn't matter whether the attention she got from men was negative or positive.

After that, Lucy began to treat herself differently. She started to change her perceptions of herself and then her behavior. She realized she had worthwhile things to say and important opinions to express. And most of all, she no longer had to hide behind the armor that said loudly, "I don't care about anything. Not even myself."

Reason #4: They've never had any success at it.

Have you ever tried to tell your partner how you feel about something, but you can't find the words to express that feeling in a way they could understand? Or, worse, you tried, but in the middle of your explanation your partner started snoring like a buffalo with sinus problems?

That might be your experience now, but it's no reason to give up. Just because one way doesn't work doesn't mean another won't.

Part of the problem with communication is that men and women in general tend to take different approaches. (Note that I said "in general.")

Men often take the approach of a journalist—presenting the facts in a straightforward fashion. Every beginning news writer knows that the most important elements of a story should be contained in the first paragraph, or the lead. Those important elements are who, what, when, where, why, and sometimes how. That's generally how many men like to communicate, and also the way they want others, including their partners, to communicate with them.

Women often take the approach of a storyteller—setting the stage, coloring it with interesting characters, and describing the scene before they get into the plot. A storyteller doesn't give away the climax of the story in the first paragraph. She wants to build suspense, tell you how everything fell into place, and lead you gradually to the big conclusion.

A man's tendency is to say, "Johnson's department store burned to the ground this afternoon." A woman's tendency is to say, "As I was leaving the office today, I thought I smelled smoke in the air. And then, sure enough, a couple of fire trucks went flying past, headed in the direction of Oak Street . . ."

Let me reiterate that I'm not saying *all* men communicate like journalists or that *all* women are storytellers. However, there is a general tendency for the genders to be divided along those lines.

If you think I'm wrong, think back over your conversations. Who is the one who usually corrects a specific version of a story by reminding their partner of elements they've "forgotten"? It's usually the woman. Funny thing is, it's more than likely those are elements the man left out on purpose to make his story more concise—another journalistic trait.

I'm not saying one approach to communication is right and the other is wrong; I'm simply highlighting the differences in

220

communication styles. With such differences, a woman may feel shortchanged because her husband isn't giving her all the interesting details she craves. The husband may be impatient and say something unkind such as, "Will you *please* get to the point?" or "I don't need all the details. Just give me the highlights. If I want to know more, I'll ask."

Communication—especially male-female communication—is a complex puzzle. That's why many couples have never learned how to communicate in a deep, meaningful way. But there are basically two reasons why we have no success at good communication: we don't listen, and we don't perceive what is being said.

Listening is at least a third of the communication process. The other two-thirds is the sharing of self and the understanding that follows the listening.

When your partner is talking to you and you're thinking about what you're going to say in response, you're not listening. You really aren't communicating because you're too busy formulating your own thoughts. This is especially true in arguments, where neither combatant is really listening to the points the other person is making. If there was more in the way of listening, there would be less in the way of disagreements. Bickering only raises the ante and creates a spirit of competition in which somebody has to win and somebody has to lose. In marriage, if one partner loses, you both lose.

Communication—especially male-female communication—is a complex puzzle. That's why many couples have never learned how to communicate in a deep, meaningful way.

Instead, when you understand how important listening is, and that styles of communication are different, you will learn to appreciate (and even chuckle at) each other's journalistic and storytelling habits.

Sande and I sure do.

Communication 101

When we first get to know someone, do we share our intimate feelings and deepest secrets? Of course not. That's because we don't know them. There are different stages of communication, and we use them unwittingly depending on how comfortable we are with the person we're talking to.

Stage 1: The Superficial Rut

Every day we pass by people on the sidewalk. Some of them we recognize because they're on the same schedule as us, but we don't really know or interact with them much. At most we share this kind of exchange:

"Good morning! Nice day, isn't it?"

"Yeah. How are you doing?"

"I'm fine."

Most of those conversations are perfunctory at best. They're nice but a bit boring, and they never get beyond the surface.

But what if, when someone asked, "How are you doing?" you said something instead of the typical "I'm fine"? Perhaps something like, "Well, thanks for asking. My hemorrhoids are really killing me." Now *that* might lead to an interesting conversation.

The point I'm trying to make is that many marriage partners, for various reasons, get into a rut where they stay superficial. They might be married for a long time yet never have the chance to get to know who the other person is. They live the single lifestyle with separate friends, separate bank accounts, separate breakfast foods, separate everything. For whatever reason, their relationship resembles more of a financial partnership or a brother-sister relationship than a heart connection.

That kind of married lifestyle is easy. It's less risky. And people get used to living in that kind of a rut. There's not much emotional connection, so it's a no-harm, no-foul existence.

It's not great, but it's okay. In fact, life is okay. You've got your job; your spouse has theirs. The kids are grown now—off to college or settled into their own lives. But your relationship is missing the vibrancy of an intimate connection that should be in every marriage.

Stage 2: The Clark Kent Phenomenon

In this level, you two become reporters for the *Great Metropolitan Newspaper*. You report on everything that happened at work, a conference you had with your kid's teacher, and what the neighbor told you the other day. It's all factual, but nothing is personal.

A Stage 2 person can talk your ear off but never tell you anything. This kind of communication might be lively, but it establishes a certain measured distance between the speaker and others, keeping the listeners at bay. It's a self-protective behavior learned over years that serves the speaker well. It also keeps them from thinking about themselves and some of the apprehension, fear, regret, and self-doubt that have crept into their life over the years. So they fill the air with words—talk about things that are inconsequential and impersonal.

Stage 3: Cautious Sharing

In this level, you risk sharing some of your ideas, thoughts, and opinions. You still are cautious, though, because you're unsure if your ideas will be met with criticism or approval. You want to avoid criticism at all costs, and it's far more comfortable for your spouse to see the ideal self you want them to see. You open your intellect but don't open your heart. After all, showing your real self would still be a bit risky.

Stage 4: Entrance of Feelings and Emotions

Sharing your feelings, as we explored earlier, can be a dicey experience, but it's a necessary one. In this stage, you begin to share the personal feelings behind your thoughts, ideas, and opinions. For many couples, this is the most intimate stage they reach.

There's a scene in the classic play *Fiddler on the Roof* in which Tevye wants his wife, Golde, to tell him she loves him. To his question of "Do you love me?" she replies with a list of all the things she's done for him in their years of marriage. She's mended his clothes, she's cooked his meals, she's done this and that. Still he persists, "Do you love me?"

Actions are wonderful in showing your partner you care. But they are not enough. Ever.

Actions are wonderful in showing your partner you care. But they are not enough. Ever. Those innermost feelings of love and appreciation need to be voiced. Like Tevye, your partner needs to hear how much you love them. They also need to know when something frustrates or angers you.

It isn't easy to share your deepest emotions and feelings with another person—even if that person is someone you love. But I encourage you to take steps in that direction, little by little. Don't just stay at this stage. Take it to the next one.

Stage 5: Unconditional Trust and Open Communication

If you want a deeply intimate connection, this is the stage you work toward. In this stage, both partners trust each other so deeply that they can share anything with each other—positive or negative—in a spirit of love. They know, "I can tell you how I really feel without you judging that feeling."

Many couples struggle to get to this level of communication because of the possibility of being rejected. This stage isn't easy to reach—it takes time and dedication. But let me tell you, it's worth it.

One note, though. If God Almighty wanted us to know everything our partner thinks and feels, he would have given us all glass foreheads. In other words, don't push your spouse to reveal what they're not ready to reveal. We all have different comfort-ability levels. What's important is that we don't question or judge but empathize with the hurt, and that we support our spouse.

How to Say "I Love You" So Your Spouse Hears It

I'm the gopher in our family. I get all the good assignments.

"Honey, would you go to the nursery and buy me some black gold?" Sande asks me.

"Some what?" I ask.

"Black gold," she says, as if that explains everything I need to know.

"They sell gold at the nursery?" I scratch my head. "We have that kind of money?"

She sighs. "No, honey. It's a soil, and they call it black gold because it's rich in nutrients."

"Oh, gotcha."

Then, like the wonderful husband I am, I scurry off to the nursery to bring home the black gold.

When I tote that bag out of the car trunk and drag it toward the green-thumbed Mrs. Uppington, her five-foot-nine-inch body is already leaning over in anticipation. She takes great care in making sure all her plants are nestled nicely in that soil and watered well. She always ends up with beautiful flowers, plants, and trees. That result isn't due to happenstance or good luck. It's because Sande carefully cultivates the ground so that the flower or plant or tree can live up to its potential.

Every day you have opportunities to enrich your marital plant. For most women, your words are like the black gold that allows a plant to grow. What comes out of your mouth can be a nutrient, a weed killer, or a marital killer. Which one it ends up being is up to you. Your tongue and how you choose to use it will, on a daily basis, tell your spouse how much you really care.

Everyone has emotional sweet spots, and there's nothing better than being stroked in those spots. But your sweet spots are likely to be different from your partner's. Stroke each other in the right spots and you'll be purring like kittens. Stroke each other in the wrong spots and you'll be like a cat who has his fur rubbed the wrong way—that's a very unhappy cat.

Everyone has emotional sweet spots. But your sweet spots are likely to be different from your partner's.

In order for your spouse to receive the love you're sending and for you to receive the kind of love you need, you have to understand a few basics about how people give and receive love. I'm so thankful for my friend Gary Chapman's work on the five love languages.[1] It gives us a handle to understand that people express love differently . . . just like my *Birth Order Book* gives parents the ability to get behind their children's eyes since cubs that come out of the same den still view life completely different.

Emotional Tenderness and Touch

Some people love to have their hair stroked. Others love to hold hands. Mrs. Uppington loves to have her back scratched in an S shape (but *only* in an S shape—she is a firstborn, after all). If touch is your sweet spot, just be aware that timing is important.

"You want to hear some more bad news?" my daughter Hannah asked me one day when I got home from work.

I already knew an upstairs toilet had malfunctioned, necessitating a call to the plumber and a major cleanup in the bathroom. Then Hannah told me that the sewage had seeped downstairs into a closet, ruining some clothes, toys, and the carpet.

Obviously Sande had been having a bad day. But later that night, the plumber was gone, the carpets were pried up so the floor underneath could dry, and the fans were blowing. The house still smelled pretty aromatic, but we could finally relax a little.

The kids were over at a friend's house for a belated dinner while we cleaned up.

Sande grabbed her nightly cup of coffee and vegged out in the easy chair. Half an hour later I sauntered into the room and said, as only a dumb husband can say to a wife after such a day, "You wanna fool around?" I plastered my best Bullwinkle the Moose look on my face. How could she resist me?

Sande's eyes popped open. She shot me a glare. "Do I look like I want to fool around?"

Yes, even I, the expert, discovered that there is a time and place for intimacy, and it certainly isn't when your wife has been in the thick of sewer water all day.

I also discovered in another instance that there are huggers and non-huggers. Huggers will hug anything that moves. Non-huggers specialize in arm's-length relationships and don't want to let anything—except maybe the pillow they sleep on—get close to them.

We men are particularly prone to be non-huggers. In general, the port into our heart tends to be tightly closed. When we do allow someone in, the narrow passageway is only about two inches wide. If anyone comes roaring up with a big, loud engine on an emotional boat, good luck. Our port is going to close immediately.

> *Even I, the expert, discovered that there is a time and place for intimacy, and it certainly isn't when your wife has been in the thick of sewer water all day.*

However, approach us softly and tenderly—in a small canoe or even doing the dog paddle—and you'll ease your way right into that harbor and have no problem landing at our port.

Caring Words

If you're a person with this sweet spot, you love to hear caring, sensitive words. Verbal appreciation is very important to you. Compliments and encouraging words are the peanut butter in your PB&J. They make your world stick together. If you hear your spouse talk about your generosity and helpfulness in front of friends, you puff up like a happy peacock. You also tend to be at ease with words yourself and express yourself well.

Time and Presence

Saying "I love you" is as simple as spending time with your partner. But there's a difference between just sitting there like a couch potato and completely being present with that person. Your partner knows when you are and aren't paying attention.

If time and presence is your partner's sweet spot, make sure you do things together—go on trips, out to dinner, Rollerblading, shopping, backpacking, whatever. If this person gets time with you, he or she will be a very happy dude or dudette.

What *you do* is secondary, as long as you're doing it together.

When you think about it, it's like dating—you're spending time together to get to know each other. *What* you do is secondary, as long as you're doing it together. Spending quality time together and having quality conversation is more than a weather report. It requires involvement, eye contact, full attention—in other words, active listening. You listen for feelings and watch body language.

Soul-to-soul connections can't happen without spending time together, and a lot of it.

Surprises and Gifts

Babies of the family can be particularly prone to this one. I swear half of the bling in the world is purchased by babies of the family. I myself have a jewel-studded watch to show for it. But these surprises don't always have to be about money. A wildflower picked by the roadside because you thought of that special person means just as much. That's because it's a visual representation of your love for them.

Certain types of people gravitate to this sweet spot. They tend to be artistic but down-to-earth. Their homes are filled with mementos—a drawing on the refrigerator door, a vase from dear Aunt Edna, a trophy from high school. The gifts are not nearly as important as the meanings behind them. Each item is physical evidence of the love involved.

Each item is physical evidence of the love involved.

I'm married to a world-class gift giver. Sande even *invents* reasons to give gifts, which are always impeccably wrapped. The night before we're having friends over for dinner, she'll bake heart-shaped cookies to place in party favors that our guests can take home.

I don't have the same gift-giving nature. I figure we're already giving them dinner, so why can't *I* eat the cookies? And because of one of my sweet spots—time and presence—I'm a little bothered that she's baking for our friends instead of coming to bed with me. But I've learned to respect her sweet spot of giving, even though I don't share it. I've also learned that she loves to *receive* meaningful gifts, which means I have to give them.

Guys, never give your wife a toaster. I'm telling you from experience. And wives, don't give your husband a weed wacker unless he specifically asks for one. Gifts like that just say, "Get to work." They don't communicate love. Good gift giving requires that we look behind our spouse's eyes to see what they want and need.

Acts of Provision

Being supported emotionally, physically, and financially and feeling stable and secure are very important to some of us.

In any relationship, there are things that you just do—they're part of being a couple and sharing household responsibilities. It's nice when you receive a thank-you for doing normal chores, but you don't expect it. But if your sweet spot is acts, then it's the *extra* acts of service that you do for love, expecting extra love in return.

He always prepares dinner, but tonight he makes your favorite dessert. That's extra.

She always cleans the bathroom, but today she cleans the kitchen too, even though that's normally his job. That's extra.

She washes his car. He makes her breakfast in bed. He's sick as a dog, so she waits on him hand and foot for three days. She's headed off on a business trip and busy with last-minute preparations, so he types up her report.

None of those are normal chores. They're extras. And this is how many husbands and wives show their love.

But not all of them. Some spouses are service challenged. Not doing acts of love for each other in marriage can cause great problems, especially if only one of the partners' sweet spots is acts of love.

Here's something about acts of love. When you do them as little surprises for each other, no one loses out, even if that isn't their sweet spot.

For example, Mrs. Uppington is a very capable woman. She reared five children with me and also had her own retail store. She loves to go shopping in Phoenix, Arizona, which is 100 miles from our home. Such a shopping trip requires a hotel reservation because it's a couple-day excursion for her.

Is she capable of making her own reservation? Of course. She has the number of the hotel where she usually stays scribbled on the back of the calendar on our fridge. But she feels especially cared for when I make that reservation for her . . . even without her asking.

Basic courtesies never go out of style.

Basic courtesies, such as opening the door for your wife or calling and asking your husband if he needs anything while you're at the store, never go out of style. In the whirl of life, it's important that you don't forget them. But it's also important to remember what your spouse's primary sweet spot is, and make sure you go out of your way to give them love in the way they best receive it.

When Sweet Spots Clash

Clashes come when spouses don't understand each other's sweet spots and have different ones. In fact, it's rare that a couple shares the same sweet spots. If one of you has the sweet spot of time and presence and the other has emotional tenderness and touch, you're one lucky couple!

However, if time and presence are important to you, but surprises and gifts are important to your spouse, is it any wonder that he's out shopping for your anniversary gift when all you want is for him to be home for a simple anniversary dinner of tacos? Or if words are your sweet spot, but your husband's is providing for you and he's too tired at night to even talk, wouldn't you feel a little resentful?

Scenario #1: Will and Jillian

Will and Jillian were a very loving couple, but one issue always caused them problems. They couldn't put their finger on the root cause until they realized what their sweet spots were. Here's what happened one night that sparked their investigation of their sweet spots.

After dinner, Will told Jillian, "Great meal, honey. You're such a good cook." He kissed her on the cheek.

"Thanks," she said, "but I've got a ton of stuff to do before that meeting tonight. I have to wash the dishes, make the sandwiches for tomorrow, call Carol and Kathy about Saturday, and help Tyler learn his lines for the school play."

"When's the meeting?" he asked, as any sensitive partner would.

"In half an hour," she said, already running water for the dishes.

"I guess you have your work cut out for you. But you'll do it. I know you can," he said sweetly. "I'll be out working on the car." And off he went, leaving her with a ton of things to do in a short amount of time.

What was Will's sweet spot? Caring words. He was always very encouraging to his overworked wife. But Jillian's sweet spot was acts of provision—serving her husband, her child, and the community. She was miffed that he wasn't pitching in to help.

Meanwhile, later he was bothered that she didn't show any appreciation for the work he put into polishing the car—the very SUV that she ended up driving to the meeting. He wanted affirming words, which he didn't get.

Did they love each other? Absolutely. But they had very different ways of showing it.

Scenario #2: Dan and Janet

Dan wanted to get Janet a particular necklace for her birthday. He drove through three counties to find a store with the perfect one. When he finally found it, he was excited. All the searching was worth it, because he wanted to show his deep love for her with this extravagant gift.

Problem was, they'd invited friends over for dinner. With all the running around, Dan got home about two minutes before the guests arrived.

Janet was hustling around the kitchen when Dan burst in. She shot him an icy glare since he was supposed to have been there helping out.

In the after-thrill of the birthday gift chase, he didn't notice "the look." He was all hugs and kisses because he'd accomplished his purpose. "Sorry I'm late, but I have a great reason. Wait until you see it."

Though he'd planned to give her the gift later, he gleefully placed the nicely wrapped gift on the kitchen counter.

"What's that?" she asked, eyeing the gift skeptically.

"Open it."

"I've got to get ready."

"Open it!"

"I can't!" she protested. "The place is still a mess. I've had to do all this myself."

"I know," he cooed. "But open it, please. I went to a lot of trouble for this."

"Later," she barked, and went to find the vacuum cleaner.

Throughout dinner, they put on their best faces for the company's sake, but both were hurting. Dan wanted credit for working so hard to find the gift, which Janet wouldn't even open. Janet was peeved because Dan had left her alone to prepare dinner for guests on her own birthday. He'd said he'd be home early to help, no later than 4:00, but he'd been late.

What do you think their sweet spots are?

Yup, you're right. Dan's is surprises and gifts. Janet's is acts of provision.

Indeed, there are different strokes for different folks. What you like to receive isn't always what your spouse likes to give. What you like to give isn't always what your spouse likes to receive. Such clashes are why it's so important to know what your own sweet spot is and what your partner's is. If you want your spouse to feel your love, you have to talk in such a way that they'll hear what you're saying.

WHAT IS YOUR **SWEET SPOT?**

Identify your sweet spot and your partner's (one of them or a combination):

- Emotional tenderness and touch
- Caring words
- Time and presence
- Surprises and gifts
- Acts of provision

Did your spouse's sweet spot surprise you in any way? If so, how? How will this knowledge affect the way you give love to your spouse now? In what ways does this change the way you receive the love your spouse gives you?

How to Talk He/She Language

If you want to communicate, you have to first know who you're talking to.

We've already talked about the fact that *generally* men are journalists in their verbal style, and *generally* women are storytellers. So if you're talking to a man, you better be concise and you better have a point. If your prologue is too long, you'll lose him. If you want to get his attention, give him the CliffsNotes version first. Say, "This is important. I've got a real problem, and I think you can help me solve it." Believe me, that man will sit up and pay attention.

If you're talking to a woman, settle in and enjoy the ride. You'll learn a new vocabulary, experience a colorful swath of feelings that you never even knew was on the horizon, and glimpse details along the way that you'd never see otherwise. So appreciate and value her for who she is and for doing what you don't naturally do. Be her companion, risk sharing your heart and feelings with her, and you'll have her purring like a kitten.

If you're talking to a man, you better be concise and you better have a point. If you're talking to a woman, settle in and enjoy the ride.

And don't forget to celebrate those differences between you. A sense of humor helps.

Recently Sande and I were going on a trip. I'd rented a smaller car, so I'd asked her to pack only one bag. Well, the morning we were due to leave for the airport, I saw *two* bags of hers at the front door.

I sighed. "I'll make this real simple." I pointed to the bags. "There's one bag, and the bag next to it I'll call number two."

She pointed to the first bag and said, as only Mrs. Uppington can, "Honey, that's my bag." Then she pointed to bag number two. "And that's for my shoes."

I guess I hadn't been specific enough in my terminology.

234

Your loved one will whisk you into a new world of language that will take you a lifetime to master. It'll be a roller-coaster ride at times, but it certainly won't be boring.

What She Says versus What She Means

Sande speaks a language that took me a good 10 years of knowing her to understand—and I still haven't mastered it in spite of the fact that we now have four grandchildren.

It's like this. Men are straightforward. What they say is what they mean. You don't have to wonder. Grunts and nods even serve as weighty conversation tools.

But women say things they don't really mean, and you need to be on your toes to translate such women-speak. Here are some things many males learn the hard way:

What she says: "Do you want to stop for ice cream?"

What he says: "No thanks."

What she means: "I have an intense craving for ice cream, so you better stop right now, buster, if you know what's good for you."

Result: Uh-oh, you're in trouble if you didn't catch that one. The atmosphere in your car is soon going to resemble the ice in that ice cream . . . or she'll cry. You're not sure which is worse.

What she says: "What time are you going to be home?"

What he says: "I don't know. Probably sometime after 6:00."

What she means: "I need to know exactly what time you're going to be home. I planned a surprise, and it will be ruined if you show up early or late."

Result: If you're late, you're dead, and if you're early, you're going to miss the one time your bride manages to send the kids to Grandma's for the evening and dresses up in a new nightie she bought just for you.

What she says: "Do I look good in this dress?"

What he says: "Yeah." (And then he goes on with what he's doing.)

What she means: "I'm feeling fat, and I need you to tell me I still look pretty to you."

Result: I don't think a single male on the planet could find a win-win answer to that question, so simply accept that fact. Good luck, buddy.

See where trouble might brew if the woman doesn't say what she really means, and the male responds without realizing what she really means?

How to Get Him to Listen

Men can be as dumb as mud when it comes to interpreting women-speak. Instead of expecting your guy to be a mind reader—knowing your needs and desires by osmosis—why not gently tell him? Sure, you'd rather he just knew, but since he doesn't, who better than you to train him how you think and feel?

The woman is generally the relational guru in the relationship. If you're a typical female and your partner is a typical male, you'll use three and a half times the amount of words that he uses every day. That means when you see each other after work, you'll still have some word count left, whereas he's used up most of his daily word count in the context of his workday.

Ladies, that's when you'll do well to understand the basic concept of division. Divide carefully the number of words you choose to use with that man of yours. Think the economy plan, not the supersize plan. Perk his interest first, and he'll ask for more when he's ready. And if you make your point without excess emotions (tears really do scare men) and without being accusatory, his defenses won't kick in and block his hearing.

Five Communication Tips That Work Every Time . . . with Any Gender

How can you best communicate with the one you love?

First, learn how to listen. Listening is key to hearing what your partner is saying. Add in watching body language and eye expressions, and you'll become a pro at reading your spouse.

Second, use empathetic words. Say, "Honey, I know you're not a talker by nature. I've known you for 19 years, and sharing your feelings has never been something you've delighted in. But I want to tell you how privileged I feel to take a look into your heart and mind this afternoon." Or, "I know it's hard for you to open up and be vulnerable. I understand. But when I see tears in your eyes and know it's coming from your heart, I want to know what's bothering you, because I'd like to help."

Third, own up to your own shortcomings before you ask your spouse to change their behavior. If you do so, they will listen more attentively. Remember that sharing feelings—using "I" instead of "you" language—will pull you closer together, while judgments will push you apart.

Fourth, keep your interactions as positive as possible. Even difficult things can be said with gentleness and love. "Honey, it's important for me to please you and meet your needs. When X happens, I feel sad and wonder if I have a place in your life." As the wise old apostle Paul said centuries ago, "Love is very patient and kind, never jealous or envious, never boastful or proud, never haughty or selfish or rude. Love does not demand its own way."[2]

Fifth, commit to work together on the issue you're addressing. Marriage is the union of two people who are of equal social value. It's a 100/100 proposition. That means even when you don't understand your partner, you still do your best to translate what they're saying.

I still can't always translate Sande-speak, but I've certainly improved. Now when Sande eyes my outfit as I'm going out the door and says, "Oh, that's an interesting combination you have on, Leemie," I know immediately what that means: "You didn't dress right. Please go back and change."

And I do so, as the dutiful husband I am.

You see, I know there are some things about my lovely bride that won't change. They're a part of her personality. (Someday I'll be at my own funeral, laid out in my casket, and she'll be peering over the casket, saying, "Leemie, you're not wearing that.") But because I love that woman, I change clothes when she asks me to. It's a small thing in the scheme of our marriage, but to her, it's an act of love.

Actions, Not Just Words

If you really want an intimate connection, think first of your spouse. What would he like? How would she respond? What does he need from you most right now? When you know what each other's needs are, communicate about them, and then meet those needs with acts of love, you'll have a marriage that's happier and more fulfilling than you could ever dream.

Sande and I have reared five children. It's understandable that sometimes she got tired, especially when I was on the road and couldn't physically be present to help out. That's why I decided to do something really special for her every year or so. The first time I did it, she had no clue what to expect. (I should have known better, since she's a detail-oriented firstborn who dislikes surprises.)

I took her out for a nice dinner first. She was glowing.

Then I drove to a hotel. When I pulled up to it, she swiveled in the passenger seat and stared at me. "Leemie, just *what* are you doing?"

When I told her I wanted us to go inside, she protested, "But I don't have any luggage."

Finally, I coaxed her out of the car—make that *half carried her*—and through a side entrance. She was worried about how it would look if we went in without luggage. (See? My wife thinks of all the angles that would never enter my brain.)

When I pulled out a room key, she resisted again. Clearly she was in no mood for the hanky-panky she thought I had in mind.

She had no idea that I had been there earlier that day to reserve the room and then prepare it myself. I'd placed five pink roses—one for each of our kids—beside the bed, and two books she'd been dying to read on the nightstand.

I'd also packed a suitcase with one of her favorite nightgowns, toiletries, and a couple sets of comfy clothes and stashed it in the closet. When I brought it out, she stared at it, speechless.

I told her to relax, take a hot bath, and enjoy some reading and a good night's sleep. I said I'd order some room service on the way out—the most gooey, chocolatey thing on the menu, as well as some coffee since Sande has night-owl qualities. I told her I'd pick her up the next morning for breakfast (which, in Sande's language, means about two in the afternoon).

Then I did something that would be hard for any red-blooded male to do. I left my gorgeous wife by herself in a hotel room with a king-size bed. I kissed the woman I loved good night and walked out that door.

Why did I do that instead of staying with her and having time sans kids? Because I knew what Sande needed most at that moment—time alone, just for her. It was the most loving gift I could give her.

What might your spouse appreciate most?

BONUS SECTION

3-1-1 Couple Workout

Improve listening skills and work out relational kinks with no fighting.

Before you start on your workout, settle in at a comfortable place for both of you. Make it a place that doesn't have an audience (like friends, in-laws, or kids). The goal is to talk about issues, one at a time, that each of you wishes to see improve in your relationship— whether it's more equal sharing of household responsibilities, your leisure time, openness to change, or being more creative in your romance life.

Like all workouts, start with only one issue per session for each of you. Slowly, as you build up stamina and grow to understand each other's needs and desires more, you can have more sessions. The goal is continual learning, not a single cram-for-the-exam session. Keep going and you'll have an intimate connection in no time.

Follow these steps:

1. Flip a coin to see who goes first. Set a timer for three minutes.
2. Partner 1 has three minutes to bring up an issue they'd like to see change in their marriage. Partner 2 can't interrupt while Partner 1 is talking. Partner 2 should focus on active listening—hearing the words, watching body language, and observing emotion in their partner's eyes.
3. Set the timer for one minute. Within that time, Partner 2 must reword what they heard Partner 1 say.
4. Set the timer again for one minute. Partner 1 has the opportunity to clarify anything that was not clear.

The goal of this 3-1-1 exercise? To get issues on the table and to improve listening skills in he/she language. If you take longer than that time, you might ramble and get off track. You might also dig up past situations instead of focusing on the current one.

Human nature is such that when someone says, "Hey, this is what bothers me," and it has to do with us, we become defensive and reactive and essentially work hard to cover our keisters. That's why the timer has to be set for the 3-1-1 increments.

Responses are for clarification purposes only, not to rebut. When rebutting steps into the communication workout, one or both of you stop listening, and your blood pressure skyrockets. It's tempting to say, "Hey, I don't really agree with you," but that will get you nowhere on mutually solving the problem.

What does get you somewhere? This agreement: "I will work hard to do a better job of communicating to you what my needs are, and also to understand and meet your needs."

Your spouse can't read your mind, and you can't expect them to. Neither of you inhabits the other's mind. That's why this exercise is so important—to get issues on the table that you may not otherwise bring up but are quietly simmering under the surface, unnoticed by your spouse.

At the end of the 3-1-1 workout, reverse your roles. Repeat the same steps.

Some couples even decide to record their conversations. That helps in these cases:

"What I heard you say was . . ."
"No, I didn't say that at all. I said . . ."

Before the bickering kicks off, take a time-out. Replay that recording. Maybe one of you didn't hear right, or maybe one of you didn't word the situation the way you thought, or both. Either way, you both hear the exact words again, and it's not costing you $250 an hour for a shrink. This is something you can easily do at your dining room table, with your cell phone as a recorder.

Note: This quick workout isn't designed to delve deeply into each of the topics. (You'll need separate, longer workouts for that—again, tackling one at a time.) It's intended to kick off deep, more meaningful conversation to nudge you toward greater intimacy.

SECRET #13

You Can Have the Marriage You Deserve

Seven ways to take your marriage off autopilot
and make it the best it can be.

Be honest. When you first saw the title *The Intimate Connection*, what did you think of?

Many of you, especially if you're of the male gender, thought *sex*.

Truth of the matter is, *The Intimate Connection is* about sex . . . and it's also *not* about sex. Actually, an intimate connection—understanding each other, meeting needs, communicating on a meaningful level—is the *prelude* to a great sex life. That's because sex doesn't begin in the bedroom; it begins in the kitchen.

In fact, it begins in the kitchen because there's company in the living room.

Here's what I mean. If you have friends over, hanging out in your living room, who is the one who pops up first to get them refreshments? Nine times out of ten it's the female. The male sits there like a doofus, and she does everything. But what if you were the one out of ten, and you both popped up to serve those guests and exchanged a smile and a kiss in the kitchen? How do you think your relationship might change?

Now you're getting it.

A Promising Start

As you work toward understanding each other and meeting each other's needs, there's another benefit. Research shows that, compared to couples who choose to cohabit, married couples "are more likely to survive cancer, less likely [by 14 percent!] to suffer a stroke or heart attack, less likely to develop depression and other mental illnesses, and the list goes on," reported *Psychology Today*, noting that such an advantage is likely due to better social support, more social approval, and recognition.[1]

The reasons for those health benefits and advantages have everything to do with a woman fulfilling a man's top needs (to be needed, wanted, fulfilled), and a man fulfilling a woman's top needs (affection, honest and open communication, commitment to family). Nail those and you've essentially divorce-proofed your marriage and catapulted over any hurdles to intimacy.

If your relationship feels like it's on autopilot, the following seven habits can transform what you have now into the intimate connection you're craving.

#1: Make loving your partner a daily choice.

Marriage doesn't have to be just "all it's cracked up to be." It can be better. Even cuddling or interacting with a spouse "releases the 'love hormone' oxytocin, which promotes feelings of calm and closeness."[2]

But things of true value don't usually come without some work on your part, do they? No marriage can be on autopilot. You can't

244

flick a switch and lean back and forget about it. It's not like the old friend you see at a 10-year school reunion, with whom you've exchanged only an email or two since graduation. In half an hour, you've caught up on the basics of your life and don't have anything else to say.

No, to have a healthy marriage, you have to stay at the controls, making adjustments—whether slight or large—to make it fly on the right trajectory.

The single most important thing you can do to get an intimate connection for a lifetime is to love your spouse. Every day. Not making that choice allows little temptations to sneak in—like some airbrushed body that forces you into an unwitting comparison game or a sweet comment from a coworker when you're feeling unappreciated by your spouse.

The grass is not greener on the other side of divorce. Some of you know that already, since you've been down that path with an ex. Even if you managed to climb the fence to check out the options of greener grass, you'd still have to mow it. Even more, right now there are lots of lonely people who are single or single again, gazing wistfully over the fence at your lawn.

> *Even if you managed to climb the fence to check out the options of greener grass, you'd still have to mow it.*

So choose every day to show love to your spouse. Avert your eyes. Flip the channel. Turn the page. Then look into your spouse's eyes and say, "I love you." Those three words are indeed magical, because they break down walls and will transform your marriage.

#2: Treat your partner as a gift.

A beautiful phrase is engraved inside my wedding ring: "You are my richest blessing." All these years later, that's still how I feel about Sande—and how she feels about me. I've worn that band for so long the words are probably engraved into the skin of my ring finger.

What does treating your spouse as a gift mean? It's the difference between the way you'd treat a paper plate and the way you'd treat an antique.

Let's say you're at a backyard barbecue. The burgers and potato salad are usually served on paper plates. Sometimes, if you really want to be fancy, you use wicker plate holders so the plates remain stiffer and the sauce and other condiments won't leak through and make a mess.

What do you do with those paper plates—and maybe even with those wicker plate holders—when you're done? Even the finest in that category are no treasure. They're made to be used and then thrown away. You can even use them to play Frisbee with the dog or throw them in the bonfire. No one cares. They're disposable and not of much worth.

But what about if the plates were antique ones that you'd lovingly collected? The picture would change vastly. I know that personally, because my wife is into antiques. She's collected a few rare dishes with exquisite craftsmanship and even had her own antique store for a number of years. How do you think she'd react if I brought one of those dishes out of its glass cabinet and used it for our next barbecue? "Here, Rover . . . catch!"

Are you treating your spouse like a paper plate or a rare antique?

I know for certain *I'd* be the one in the doghouse that night, and Rover would have a comfy spot in bed next to Sande.

So let me ask you this: Are you treating your spouse like a paper plate or a rare antique? Do your actions reflect your view that your partner is a person of great value?

If you adopt this perspective, many things about your marriage will change—including how you make decisions, the way you solve problems, and how you handle your spouse's or your own bad mood. It'll even change the way you handle that TV remote control.

#3: Be quick to say, "I'm sorry," and refuse to hold grudges.

It's difficult to say, "I'm sorry." Especially because none of us are comfortable with or good at admitting that we maybe could have been wrong and hurt someone else. But it's even harder to hold grudges, because doing so requires constant supervision on your behalf to keep track of them. Now *that* takes its toll.

Like the late-sixties couple who sat in my counseling office after 30 years of a distant, emotionally estranged marriage. Their story—which came out in bits and pieces amidst barbs to each other, crossed arms, and turned-away heads—was all too familiar.

The problems had all started 30 years prior, when Hank invited his then-widowed mother to live with them. He hadn't asked his wife, Zelda, for her opinion. In General Patton style, he simply announced what was going to happen and ordered her to get the place ready for Mama.

Understandably, Zelda had a problem with that. However, because Hank was a commandant general in personality, she didn't dare broach the subject with him. Instead, she tucked her anger down deep inside. It stayed there and simmered, with other events happening through the years adding to the heating cauldron.

Zelda could have made a choice at any time to openly confront her husband about his behavior, but she didn't. Instead, not wanting to rock the boat (she was a middleborn, after all), she shut down her feelings for her husband. She started to resemble a robot who did only what she considered her duties as a wife, and no more. She wouldn't tell him what she thought about anything. She didn't get upset. She was just . . . bland.

Of course, her seemingly uncaring behavior frustrated him, so he reacted in the only way he knew how—by barking more orders. Inside, he nursed his own grudges.

Their life had gone on that way for 30 years. Imagine how exhausted both felt in the endless cycle of keeping track of all those grudges and acting out those false charades.

One day, Zelda was finally pushed to the point of breaking. She yelled at the commandant general for the first time in her life. He was dumbstruck. They initially came to my office because he'd insisted on it, thinking she was going crazy.

As husband and wife shared pieces of their story and were forced to listen to each other's words, something unimaginable happened. Tears began to stream down their faces.

"I'm sorry," he said. "I'm really sorry for everything."

"I forgive you," she said.

Then suddenly they were locked in an embrace. My office was soon waterlogged.

I couldn't help but think, *Thirty years! What a waste! When the walls could have been broken down with a few words.*

I know saying "I'm sorry" and forgiving your partner for their actions isn't easy. But do you really want to wait another 30 years like this couple did? When you shove your dirty laundry under the couch, eventually you have to dig it out, air it out, and wash it. That dirty laundry won't take care of itself. It'll only grow more aromatic, and it'll be tougher to get the stains out.

When you shove your dirty laundry under the couch, eventually you have to dig it out, air it out, and wash it. That dirty laundry won't take care of itself. It'll only grow more aromatic, and it'll be tougher to get the stains out.

If you don't take care of grudges and anger, they'll find a way out somehow, even if it takes years. Think of it this way. When you're blowing up a balloon, you add a puff of air little by little. If you blow it up too much—those puffs of air stack up—it will burst and scatter little pieces all over the room. But if you let the air out bit by bit, that balloon will reach the right firmness to last for a while.

Anger is the same. If little puffs of anger grow, you may not see them for a while. But as they stack up, they will eventually burst in what seems to be a surprising venting of anger that came from nowhere. Believe me, it came from somewhere. If you can get to the root of that anger before the explosion, you're letting the air out of the balloon little by little.

If any grudges are simmering in your relationship, don't wait. Bring them out into the open, even if it's difficult.

I smiled when I watched Hank and Zelda exit the counseling room hand in hand like two newlyweds. But I wished it would have happened sooner. After that day, they still had a long way to go. He needed to work on how to treat his wife as a social equal. She needed to learn how to talk about her feelings. But the important thing is, that day Hank and Zelda gathered the courage to take the huge first step to starting a new trajectory together.

How about you?

#4: Talk every day on a meaningful level.

Whenever I'm about to get a cold, I realize I need to up my vitamin C intake. It builds up my immune system, making me stronger and less susceptible to problems. But to stay healthy, I need to take it on a *daily* basis. Human bodies don't store up vitamin C.

Just as we need a daily dose of vitamin C to stay in the best health, every marriage needs a high dose of vitamin C—communication. And it also needs to happen on a daily basis. The best way to grow closer as a couple is to share with each other feelings, thoughts, or an event you've experienced.

Every marriage needs a high dose of vitamin C— communication.

But balance is also important. If only one person is doing the sharing, resentment can grow on both sides. Follow these basics, though, and they'll serve as a good starting point.

Give time and space to slow sharers. Some people open up more easily than others. Women in general tend to be more open about their feelings and are naturally more verbal. Sometimes slow sharers need some extra time to dredge up their feelings and to identify

WHAT **FORGIVENESS** IS **NOT**

Forgiveness is not excusing or accepting bad behavior. It doesn't say, "Oh, that's all right. No problem." On the contrary, there *was* a problem—enough of one that an "I'm sorry" and an "I forgive you" were needed.

But there's a difference between *intentional* hurt and *unintentional* hurt—both in definition and in the way such hurts should be handled. *Intentional* hurt is when one person means to cause pain to another and proceeds to do so. That requires the act of forgiveness. *Unintentional* hurt is accidental and part of living on this planet together. It doesn't require the act of forgiveness, but a simple "I'm sorry that happened" would be greatly appreciated and build bridges.

Forgiveness doesn't automatically make everything hunky-dory. Pretending you're not in pain and that the offense isn't as serious as it was won't fly long-term in any relationship. It will only instill bitterness and resentment. The problem still needs to be tackled. Saying "I'm sorry; please forgive me" is simply a starter—a door opener so the offending partner can begin repairing the damage.

Forgiveness is not conditional. Offering forgiveness is not like bargaining for a deal: "I'll forgive you if . . ." It is never conditional based on the other person's response. Forgiveness is not deserved, nor is it earned.

Forgiveness should instigate change. To be truly sorry, you need to change your ways—what you did to hurt your partner in the first place. No one is perfect. The same situation may happen again. When it does, you should ask for forgiveness again. But words are empty and pointless unless your spouse sees you clearly making an effort to change.

Forgiveness doesn't mean forgetting. It's humanly impossible to *try* to forget something once it's occurred, especially if there was emotional damage. If you try to forget something, you don't drive it farther from you. You bring it closer because you focus on the very thing you're trying to forget. That's why I say, "Forgive and remember." When you remember where you were and where you are now, you can be thankful you've moved from point A to point B. So remember just enough to change your own behaviors, but choose to let go of the associated pain.

them before moving ahead. They also need a safe environment—not tense, pointing fingers—in which to share.

If your spouse is a slow sharer, don't pounce on them. Let them word their ideas just right before you respond. Otherwise you might be already on the train and down the track before they have a chance to tell you it's heading the wrong direction.

Listen as much as you speak. How much do you talk in your relationship? Fifty percent of the time? Ninety percent? If you're talking, the other person doesn't have the opportunity to interject.

If you tend to be the talker, actively focus on listening instead. And be patient. The air doesn't need to be filled with words. If you wait, you'll likely be surprised what you'll learn about your spouse.

Keep a relaxed, even tone when you approach your spouse about a problem. Nothing's more threatening than your partner saying, "We need to talk."

Your immediate gut response? *Uh-oh, what have I done now?*

Take it from someone who knows. I've been in that hot seat more than once with my wife, whom I affectionately call Mrs. Uppington because she's proper and classy. I've also been on the receiving end of those words and the quirked eyebrow that tell me I'm in trouble. I can tell you, there's nothing that makes this baby of the family freeze faster in his tracks than those words.

So how about saying instead, "Honey, when you have a minute, I'd love for us to talk about something"? A calm voice and the use of "us" go a long way toward starting off a conversation on the right foot.

Talk about life around you. Fill your spouse in on life as you experience it during the day. Texts, phone calls, laughter at dinner over an event—all those things draw you closer together. Report not only what happened but how you feel about those experiences. If you do, you'll never run out of things to talk about.

Learn about and support your partner's interests. Of course, you are your partner's greatest passion, but show interest in other things they're into. Maybe it's fly-fishing, car racing, basketball, or trying to cook the perfect crème brûlée. Even if you will never fully love those things, you can at least go along for the ride, try them out, and appreciate your spouse's efforts in that regard.

Instead of asking questions, say, "Tell me more about that." If you want to shut down someone who is quieter by nature, ask him questions. Asking why is a challenge that puts any recipient on the defensive. But saying, "Wow, that's a rough situation. Tell me more about that" opens the door for him to safely share both the situation and his feelings about it.

So ease up. Allow your partner to tell details when he's ready. Going into interrogation mode will only result in a closed clamshell. You're not the FBI, so don't operate like it.

Because you and your partner are individuals, you'll have disagreements, misunderstandings, and even differing priorities. The only way to work those out, without letting any grudges fester, is if you can talk them out on a daily basis.

"If you can't say somethin' nice, don't say nothin' at all," Bambi's mother told him in the Disney classic movie *Bambi*. It seems like pretty good advice at first glance. Before you say something damaging, think, *How can I word this so it will be helpful, not harmful, to us as a couple?*

However, there are times when you should speak up. Holding in your frustrations will only cause them to grow until there's an inevitable explosion. So take care of any friction as soon as you can.

Never air any dirty laundry in public. Keep any disagreements between the two of you. No exceptions . . . unless it's with a professional counselor. Talking with friends or family members about a problem between you and your partner only makes the issue more difficult to resolve, especially for spouses who tend to be more private and reserved.

Get the problem out in the open without pointing fingers or name-calling. Say, "I may not be interpreting this correctly, but when X happens, I feel like . . ." When you frame an issue like that, you're opening the door to healthy discussion and resolving the issue creatively to your and your spouse's mutual satisfaction.

Face each other and set a two-minute alarm on your cell phone. One person should state their perspective on what happened. When the timer goes off, it's the other person's turn for two minutes. Neither of you can interrupt the other. Setting that important rule gives you both the opportunity to view life through the other's eyes so that you understand the reasons behind the friction and can brainstorm solutions.

When your spouse is talking, focus on their eyes, their body language, and what they're really saying instead of thinking of what you'll say next. For a conversation to be effective, it has to be two-way, with two good listeners.

Stick to the subject at hand. No bone-digging of past events to ratchet up the emotion. Handle one issue at a time, as it happens.

When a problem is resolved (or even partially resolved), don't merely walk away to get to your next task. Instead, look your spouse in the eye and say, "I know that wasn't easy to talk about. But thanks for filling me in. I'm glad we could work on that together." It's even better if you give each other a hug and kiss to seal the deal.

The old proverb "Don't let the sun go down on your anger" is right on the money. If you make that one of your marriage mantras, you're a smart couple indeed.

#5: Respect your partner always—publicly and privately.

Criticism is one of the biggest killers of marriages. Hearing that you are stupid or you can't do anything right doesn't encourage you to work harder at a task. It simply breeds resentment and shuts you down.

One wife, after being told too often by her husband that she was a bad cook, went out of her way to burn his favorite pot roast every Tuesday. His criticism and her reaction to it set up a damaging cycle in their relationship.

Words can kill hearts even faster than bullets kill bodies. Even if you have a concern, speak the truth in love. Look for positive things to say that can balance out the negative things.

When criticism happens privately, it's bad enough. But it's even worse when it happens in front of friends, neighbors, and relatives. That's an embarrassment that's difficult to recover from. The one who is getting harangued is embarrassed.

Look for positive things to say that can balance out the negative things.

But the one doing the yelling and name-calling should be more embarrassed.

It's easy to complain about your spouse when you get together with "the girls" or "the boys." But when you bad-mouth them in front of others and unload frustrations that you should share with your spouse, you're damaging your marriage.

There's nothing more sweet, beautiful, and inspiring to watch than husbands and wives who speak well of each other in public. It indicates genuine and mutual respect within their marriage.

#6: Try to view life from behind your spouse's eyes, understand their needs, and meet those needs.

We've already talked about men's needs and women's needs earlier in the book. But I'm here to tell you that in the quest to do special things for your spouse, you'll sometimes have epic fails.

When I was on a business trip in Erie, Pennsylvania, I decided I wanted to buy my wife a personal surprise. So, while walking in the mall, I stumbled upon a store called Victoria's Secret. It was the first time I'd entered a place like that, and I must have looked like I just fell off the turnip truck.

I walked through the store, shuffling my feet, muttering, "Shazam!" . . . not quite knowing where to look. As I sidled along, I nearly knocked over a scantily clad mannequin.

Soon not one but *two* smiling clerks—young enough to be my own children—came out from behind the counter. One approached and said, at about 40 decibels, "Hi, sir! May I help you? Are you looking for some bras? Maybe some panties?"

Edging into a corner where I hoped I wouldn't be as visible, I said, "Uh, I'm looking for a nightie."

"Oh, we've got all kinds of nighties," she said, again at 40 decibels. "Come right on over here."

She reached toward a rack and held up an option. It was about a foot and a half long at best. I'm not kidding.

I stared at her, shaking my head. "Uh, no, that won't do. My wife is five-foot-nine, not two-foot-nine."

The young lady wasn't deterred at all by my comment. She reached back to the rack and grabbed another nightie—a long one with spaghetti straps at the shoulders. She told me it was red. I'm color-blind, so I had to take her word for it. At least I could tell it had a silky feel that would perfectly fit my elegant wife.

Ten minutes later, I stood at the Victoria's Secret counter, wallet in hand. The lass had wrapped up the nightie in some scented tissue paper and tucked it not in a box, where it would be hidden from the outside world when I carried it out, but in a fancy open bag, with crinkly paper on top and the store logo emblazoned on it.

In the meantime, the other clerk had convinced me to buy three jars of stuff to rub on your body that's supposed to smell good. Before I was done, I'd spent $120, and it was all tucked into that very girlie-looking pink bag with black tissue paper.

I walked out of that store in a nearly catatonic state. When I woke up, I felt stupid, to be honest.

A day later, I returned home late at night. My wife, who keeps the active hours of a raccoon, was still up, reading the newspaper at the kitchen table. Feeling like a fish out of water, I plunked the package down in front of her.

"What's that?" she asked.

"Oh, just a little something."

"You're so sweet." She gave me a peck on the cheek. After she opened it, there was a slight pause. Then she said, "Oh, honey, it's beautiful. I'll go take this to the bedroom."

I never saw that nightie again.

This story happened when I was 50 years old and Sande was 48. I'd written 15 books by that time, and I knew something about men and women. I also certainly knew Sande, and I should have known the kind of nightie she likes. Right then her favorite was a plaid one with legs in it. It was flannel and five-eighths of an inch thick. I've got plywood in my garage that's thinner than that.

I have no idea what she did with the red silk nightie. Maybe she gave it to Goodwill or donated it to our local BFI (the garbage pickup service). Or perhaps some guy's checking his oil with it tonight on the south side of Tucson.

Anyway, I learned a lasting lesson through that experience—to always look behind my wife's eyes when buying her something special. Instead of thinking, *What would I like to get her?* I need to think, *What would be special for her? What would she like to receive?*

The best gift you can give is to get behind your partner's eyes, to understand what they really want and need.

If you're like Sande, it's certainly not a red silk nightie.

#7: Make time for the two of you.

I have a friend who tried for over a year to grow an avocado plant. She finally succeeded with a little green sprout after months of tending multiple avocado seeds in various containers. In the weeks to follow, with all her TLC and lots of sunlight from a window, that one sprout took off like gangbusters.

Then she had to go out of town on a business trip. Five days later she returned, and that sprout didn't look so good. It had, in fact, shriveled and died. You see, that tender plant needed tending and watering every day to reach its full potential and keep on growing.

Your marriage, like that plant growing on the window ledge, needs tending and watering every day too. There are lots of things you need to do to feed it and help it grow to its potential. If you neglect that marriage plant, it suffers. Weeds grow around it. Bugs might even attack. A host of "marriage eaters" will nip away at your relationship.

I know many of you have demanding jobs and travel. I'm on the road a lot myself. Add to that family responsibilities, household tasks, and personal interests, and it's an awful lot to handle. In the midst of all that, how do you prioritize what's most important? With whom and on what do you spend your available "free" time?

With whom and on what do you spend your available "free" time?

If you're spending all your leftover time surfing the web, working late, leading a Cub Scout troop, gardening, or shopping with friends instead of spending some time with your spouse, then frustrations, false expectations, temptations, and resentment can begin to clutter your marriage. It isn't that hobbies and time with friends aren't good things. It's that time with your spouse should be your most important priority.

Some business-oriented types say that time is money. But I think time is becoming even more valuable than money in today's society. As our responsibilities increase and our schedules tighten, it's nearly impossible to squeeze anything else in. We have, in a way, almost too many choices for how to spend our time. We have to prioritize even between good things.

For instance, if both your grandma and your best friend have important social events they invite you to on the same Saturday afternoon, which event would you choose to go to? What if both those activities are happening the same day you've promised your spouse that the two of you would declutter your place? Then what would you choose?

The way you spend your time is an indication of what's most important to you—even more than how you spend your money. So take a good look at your Google calendar and what it reveals about your priorities. How much time do you spend with your partner (and kids if you have them) in comparison to everything else you're doing?

The way you spend your time is an indication of what's most important to you—even more than how you spend your money.

Some people still believe in quality time—that it doesn't matter how much time you spend together, as long as it's doing something important. Ten minutes of intense discussion beats two hours of watching TV together. At least, that's the theory.

But it's wrong. You can't get quality time without spending a quantity of time, because presence is what starts and continues the process of binding your hearts together. In fact, *both* are needed—intense discussion, relaxing downtimes, and every other kind of time in between.

You might be an electrician who works long hours or a stay-at-home dad who carpools the kids in your apartment building to school every day. You might be a VP of a local bank or work part-time from home. Well, thanks to modern technology like cell phones and email, you can keep in touch with your spouse here and there throughout your day, no matter where the two of you roam.

If your job or other responsibilities are keeping you away from your spouse for a significant portion of your time, however, now's your opportunity to carefully assess your cluttered schedule. Take a meat cleaver to it, in fact. Cut out anything that isn't absolutely necessary first (and no finagling—watching reruns of *Blue Bloods* or *Gilmore Girls* isn't necessary). Then choose *one* activity (a hobby, club, etc.) per month, quarter, or year that's most important to you to add back into your schedule. That way you retain some personal time for yourself—something we all need to regroup—yet still accomplish your purpose.

Follow those simple steps for pruning your schedule and you'll be amazed how much time you'll suddenly have to build an intimate connection with your partner.

If your work continually grows, you may also need to look at that demanding job and ask, "Is this really worth as much as my marriage?" I hope the answer is no.

Putting your foot down and telling your boss that you're not able to work extra hours every week is difficult, and it may not put you on the path to a promotion. Coworkers may initially be unhappy. You may even have to switch jobs. However, if you want to find an intimate connection with your spouse, you're not going to find it by camping out at work.

Ask any older person, "If you had to do your life over again, where would you choose to spend the majority of your time?"

I doubt they would say, "At work." Most would say, "With my family."

We all have the same amount of time. We must decide how to use it.

You and your spouse are both busy. You have a bazillion things to do. Don't let each other get lost in the shuffle.

If You're a Person of Faith . . .

If you and your spouse are people of faith, it's important that you continue growing together spiritually as well. Praying together, studying the Bible, and discussing books that address issues from a faith perspective can also deepen your intimacy as a couple.

Encourage each other to learn more about your faith and apply what you've learned to life. But also make sure that you give your partner space to grow at their natural pace. No two people will have the exact same ideas, nor will they process at the same pace. Neither of you is inferior or superior. You're just different . . . and that's a good thing.

Above all, remember the words of the second greatest commandment: "Love your neighbor as much as you love yourself."[3] That applies to everyone around you—good Samaritans and bad hombres, the folks next door, the kids who hang out in front of

7-Eleven . . . and your spouse most of all. After all, that spouse is your closest neighbor.

. . . .

Even when you try all these things, you won't be perfect. Nothing in this life is perfect. That's why we're not going for perfection; we're going for excellence.

You'll have up and down days in your marriage—even up and down years. Every couple does. Making an intimate connection with your spouse isn't easy, but it is simple. All you need is a paradigm that goes like this: "It's my job to understand my spouse and all their idiosyncrasies. To truly love them, I need to figure out what makes them tick and meet those needs in a way that communicates love to them."

Do that and you'll get the marriage you both deserve.

Conclusion

Your Intimate Connection Awaits

*Experience the mutual satisfaction and excitement
of two truly becoming one.*

"Oh, Dad, it's so cute to hear Mom describing what's going on,"
my daughter Holly told me recently, laughing.

There's nothing cute about having a flu bug, and Sande had the
beginning of a good one. But what my daughter found endearing
was what I was doing about it.

"I love the way you're buying bananas to make sure she gets
enough potassium and baking potatoes so that you make sure she
has a snack she can eat," Holly said, then added a litany of other
things I'd said to my wife.

Now that's good pass-along gossip, ladies and gentlemen. I felt
good because my wife felt so treasured by me that she'd shared
the sweet things I was doing for her. But most of all, I was happy
because I was taking care of Sande, and I knew by how she'd
responded—telling our daughter about it—that I'd met her needs.

You see, marriage should be a union of two people walking in the same direction and supporting each other. Note that I said *two people*, not clones. You won't be and shouldn't be clones of each other. It truly is those differences that make you a couple. As I said earlier, if both of you are the same, there's no need for one of you.

So what does a good marriage look like?

Essentially it's like a business partnership without your clothes on. You've made a mutual agreement to be by each other's side and gone through some steps and likely some paperwork to get there. You have a mutual goal and are working together to get there. Like all businesses, there are checks and balances—areas where you are strong and your partner is weak, and vice versa, and the two of you need to support each other. What's wonderful about that situation is that you end up realizing you need each other. Frankly, you're at your best *with* each other, and at a loss without each other. Being without your spouse would be like losing your editor at a publishing company or losing your accountant at the bank.

> **What does a good marriage look like? Essentially it's like a business partnership without your clothes on.**

Your relationship is cemented with the mortars of trust, truthfulness, honor, respect, kindness, and above all, honest, transparent, straightforward communication. Transparency with each other means you never lie to each other. You don't hide anything. You aren't afraid to tell each other who you really are. That means sharing burdens, fears, dreams, and any concerns without fear that your partner will judge you or lose respect for you.

When people get hurt once in a relationship, they begin to keep things inside. Some give up and accept the way it is: *I'll just pay my dues, avoid conflict, say and do things I don't really mean, and somehow survive.*

They're right. They will survive. But their marriage won't thrive. Each spouse will start or continue living a married-singles lifestyle.

You can see those types of married singles everywhere. Look around at the couples at a restaurant sometime. How many are engaged in conversation? How many don't say a word to each other while they eat?

Sande and I have been married for over 50 years—in a row. We always find plenty to say to each other while we eat. That's because we've both worked to understand each other's needs, meet those needs, and communicate regularly about issues close to our hearts. People in good marriages service each other. They think of the other first.

It's like the salesclerk who asks, "How can I help you?" when you walk in the door. That's a good start for any marital conversation too.

Many men and women today are caught up in "equality." Well, in marriage, equality is only about treating each other with respect as human beings. It isn't about making sure everything—housework, jobs, finances—is even-steven. Equality isn't about dividing chores; it's about respecting each other in all decisions. And it certainly doesn't allow for selfishness, conceit, or trying to get the upper hand on each other.

> *People in good marriages service each other. They think of the other first.*

Each of you has grown up in different environments. If you're newly married, it'll take a while to adjust. Even if you've been married for a while, you may not have thought about how your partner's background, personality, and birth order affects them. Now that you know, how will you respond the next time you two clash? Communication is about truly listening, thinking from each other's perspective, and then coming to a compromise where you both are mutually satisfied.

Two truly *can* become one, so why not experience what a committed, exciting marriage can be like? You've got all the tools now, so it's up to you. Why not take the "I Promise" Challenge on page 265?

If you're ready for that but your spouse isn't, don't push. Take the challenge yourself. Remember, if you want to change your spouse, try changing yourself first. You'll be amazed what even little steps will do to transform your marriage.

When you change your responses, your spouse will wonder, *How come she reacted differently to me this time when I said that?* Before long, he'll be curious and alert.

In one of Aesop's fables, a tortoise competes with a hare and wins a race. Unlike the hare, he didn't jump the gun at the starting line. He didn't get impatient with the delays and sidetracks along the way and try to race to the finish line. Instead, his philosophy was, "Slow and steady wins the race."

The same is true in marriage. No transformation—especially changes in your relationship—will happen instantly. But with the principles and suggestions in this book, you can move from a rut-like, day-to-day coexistence to a vibrant relationship where you can't wait to see what happens next—from boring conversations to meaningful exchanges, from blah interactions to playful ones, from cold wars to passionate embraces, and so much more.

"Slow and steady wins the race."

No matter what the rest of the world (in-laws, friends, exes) throws at you, you'll be able to face it together. That's because you'll be soul mates—friends and lovers who love each other as you really are.

Now *that's* the intimate connection that will last for a lifetime.

The "I Promise" Challenge

I promise . . .

- To make loving you a daily choice.
- To treat you as a gift.
- To be quick to say, "I'm sorry," and refuse to hold grudges.
- To talk with you every day on a meaningful level.
- To respect you always—publicly and privately.
- To try to view life from behind your eyes, understand your needs, and meet them.
- To make time for just us.

Notes

Secret #2 Outside Forces Have Shaped Your Relationship (without Your Permission)

1. Aaron Ben-Zeév, "Does Cohabitation Lead to More Divorces?" *Psychology Today*, March 28, 2013, https://www.psychologytoday.com/us/blog/in-the-name -love/201303/does-cohabitation-lead-more-divorces.

2. Ben-Zeév, "Cohabitation."

3. Lauren Fox, "The Science of Cohabitation: A Step toward Marriage, Not a Rebellion," *Atlantic*, March 20, 2014, https://www.theatlantic.com/health/archi ve/2014/03/the-science-of-cohabitation-a-step-toward-marriage-not-a-rebellion /284512/.

4. Ben-Zeév, "Cohabitation."

5. Ben-Zeév, "Cohabitation."

6. Ben-Zeév, "Cohabitation."

Secret #3 Preconceived Notions Matter

1. For more tips on becoming a new you, see my book *Have a New You by Friday*.

Secret #6 Sex Is Important . . . but Not for the Reasons You Might Think

1. For some great and easy reads on improving your sex life together, check out *Have a New Sex Life by Friday* and *Sheet Music*. You'll be glad you did.

Secret #7 To Love Your Spouse, You Have to Know Who You Married

1. For more on birth order, see *The Birth Order Book*.

Secret #8 Clashes Feel Less Personal When You Understand Your Partner's Personality

1. Live Science Staff, "Personality Set for Life by 1st Grade, Study Suggests," *Live Science*, August 6, 2010, https://www.livescience.com/8432-personality-set-life-1st-grade-study-suggests.html.
2. Live Science Staff, "Personality Set for Life."
3. "The Four Temperaments," Fish Eaters, accessed September 29, 2018, http://www.fisheaters.com/fourtemperaments.html.

Bonus Section Want to Better Understand Your Spouse?

1. For more on understanding early childhood memories, see my book *What Your Childhood Memories Say About You.*

Secret #10 Feelings Pull You Together; Judgments Push You Apart

1. Ephesians 4:26.

Secret #12 For Your Spouse to Truly Hear You, You Have to Talk in a Way That Encourages Them to Listen

1. Discover your love language through Gary D. Chapman's *The 5 Love Languages*, 2nd ed. (Chicago: Northfield Publishing, 1995). For more information on the five love languages, visit https://www.5lovelanguages.com/.
2. 1 Corinthians 13:4–5.

Secret #13 You Can Have the Marriage You Deserve

1. Neel Burton, "Are Married People Healthier?" *Psychology Today*, June 11, 2017, https://www.psychologytoday.com/us/blog/hide-and-seek/201706/are-married-people-healthier.
2. Burton, "Are Married People Healthier?"
3. Matthew 22:39.

About Dr. Kevin Leman

An internationally known psychologist, radio and television personality, speaker, educator, and humorist, **Dr. Kevin Leman** has taught and entertained audiences worldwide with his wit and common-sense psychology.

The *New York Times* bestselling and award-winning author of over 50 titles, including *The Birth Order Book*, *Making Children Mind without Losing Yours*, *Have a New Kid by Friday*, and *Sheet Music*, has made thousands of house calls through radio and television programs, including *FOX & Friends*, Hallmark Channel's *Home & Family*, *The View*, FOX's *The Morning Show*, *Today*, *Morning in America*, *The 700 Club*, CBS's *The Early Show*, CNN, and *Focus on the Family*. Dr. Leman has served as a contributing family psychologist to *Good Morning America* and frequently speaks to schools, CEO groups, and businesses, including Fortune 500 companies and others such as YPO, Million Dollar Round Table, and Top of the Table.

Dr. Leman's professional affiliations include the American Psychological Association, SAG-AFTRA, and the North American Society of Adlerian Psychology. He received the Distinguished Alumnus Award (1993) and an honorary Doctor of Humane Letters degree (2010) from North Park University; and a bachelor's degree in psychology, and later his master's and doctorate degrees, as well as the Alumni Achievement Award (2003), from the University of Arizona. Dr. Leman is the founder and chairman of the board of Leman Academy of Excellence (www.lemanacademy.com).

Originally from Williamsville, New York, Dr. Leman and his wife, Sande, live in Tucson, Arizona, and have five children and four grandchildren.

If you're looking for an entertaining speaker for your event or fund-raiser, or for information regarding business consultations, webinars, or the annual "Wit and Wisdom" cruise, please contact:

Dr. Kevin Leman
PO Box 35370
Tucson, Arizona 85740
Phone: (520) 797-3830
Fax: (520) 797-3809
www.birthorderguy.com
www.drleman.com

Follow Dr. Kevin Leman on Facebook (facebook.com/DrKevin Leman) and on Twitter (@DrKevinLeman). Check out the free podcasts at birthorderguy.com/podcast.

Resources by Dr. Kevin Leman

Nonfiction Books for Adults

The Birth Order Book
Have a New Kid by Friday
Have a New Husband by Friday
Have a New Teenager by Friday
The Way of the Shepherd (written with William Pentak)
Have a New You by Friday
Have a New Sex Life by Friday
Have a Happy Family by Friday
Planet Middle School
The Way of the Wise
Be the Dad She Needs You to Be
What a Difference a Mom Makes
Parenting the Powerful Child
Under the Sheets
Sheet Music
Making Children Mind without Losing Yours
It's Your Kid, Not a Gerbil!

Born to Win

The Intimate Connection

7 Things He'll Never Tell You . . . But You Need to Know

What Your Childhood Memories Say about You

Running the Rapids

Becoming the Parent God Wants You to Be

Becoming a Couple of Promise

A Chicken's Guide to Talking Turkey with Your Kids about Sex (written with Kathy Flores Bell)

First-Time Mom

Step-parenting 101

Living in a Stepfamily without Getting Stepped On

The Perfect Match

Be Your Own Shrink

Stopping Stress before It Stops You

Single Parenting That Works

Why Your Best Is Good Enough

Smart Women Know When to Say No

Fiction: The Worthington Destiny Series, with Jeff Nesbit

A Perfect Ambition

A Powerful Secret

A Primary Decision

Books for Children, with Kevin Leman II

My Firstborn, There's No One Like You

My Middle Child, There's No One Like You

My Youngest, There's No One Like You

My Only Child, There's No One Like You

My Adopted Child, There's No One Like You

My Grandchild, There's No One Like You

DVD/Video Series for Group Use

Have a New Kid by Friday

Making Children Mind without Losing Yours (parenting edition)

Making Children Mind without Losing Yours (public school teacher edition)

Value-Packed Parenting

Making the Most of Marriage

Running the Rapids

Single Parenting That Works

Bringing Peace and Harmony to the Blended Family

DVDs for Home Use

Straight Talk on Parenting

Why You Are the Way You Are

Have a New Husband by Friday

Have a New You by Friday

Have a New Kid by Friday

Available at 1-800-770-3830
www.birthorderguy.com
www.drleman.com

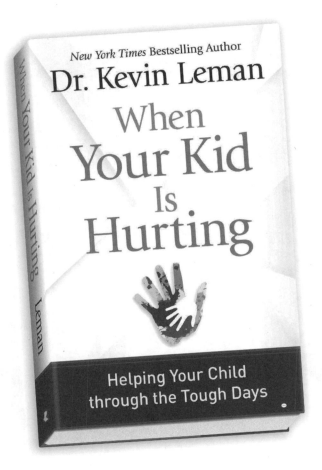

Take the
5-day challenge

Family expert Dr. Kevin Leman reveals in this *New York Times* bestseller why your kids do what they do, and what you can do about it—**in just 5 days.**

Kid-tested,
parent-approved

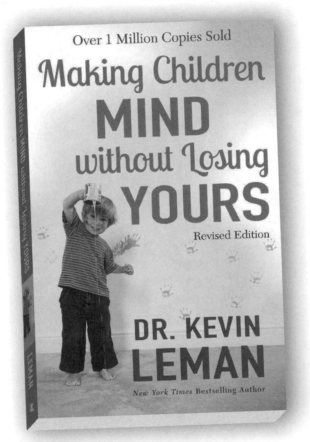

If anyone understands why children behave the way they do, it's Dr. Kevin Leman. In this bestseller he equips parents with seven principles of reality discipline—a loving, no-nonsense parenting approach that really works.

You are about to embark on a fantastic journey.

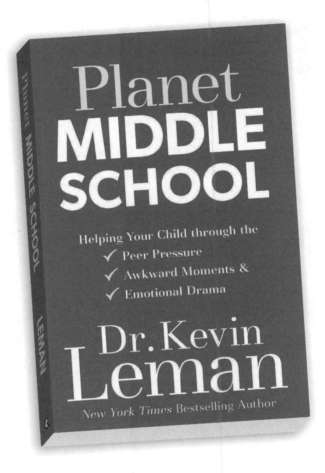

Middle schoolers can be a strange, unpredictable species. But with a little help from Dr. Kevin Leman, you can ride out the interstellar storm with humor and confidence. He will show you how you can help your child not only survive but thrive during these turbulent years.

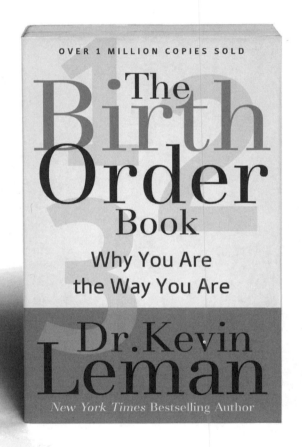

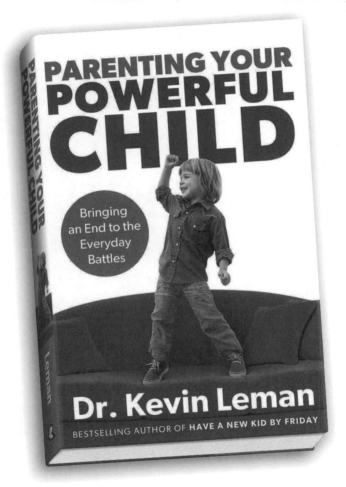

Visit BirthOrderGuy.com
for more information, resources, and videos from Dr. Kevin Leman's popular books.

Follow Dr. Leman on

 Dr Kevin Leman

 drleman